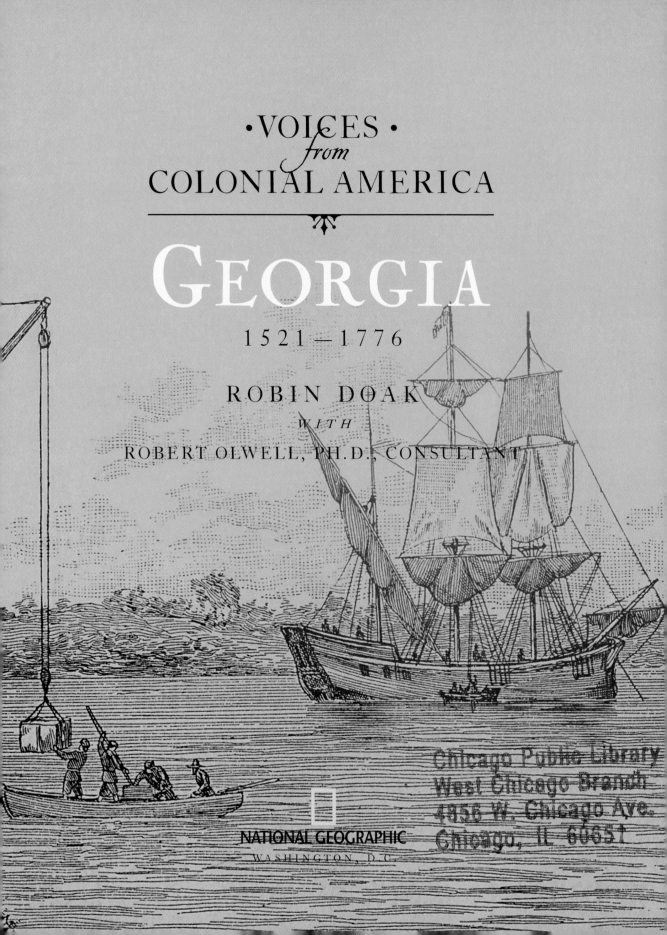

· VOICES ·
from
COLONIAL AMERICA

GEORGIA

1521 — 1776

ROBIN DOAK

WITH

ROBERT OLWELL, PH.D., CONSULTANT

NATIONAL GEOGRAPHIC
WASHINGTON, D.C.

Text copyright © 2006 National Geographic Society
Published by the National Geographic Society.
All rights reserved. Reproduction of the whole or any part of the contents without written permission from the National Geographic Society is strictly prohibited. For information about special discounts for bulk purchases, please contact National Geographic Books Special Sales: ngspecsales@ngs.org

John M. Fahey, Jr., *President and Chief Executive Officer*
Gilbert M. Grosvenor, *Chairman of the Board*
Nina D. Hoffman, *Executive Vice President,*
  President of Books and Education Publishing Group
Ericka Markman, *Senior Vice President, President of*
  Children's Books and Education Publishing Group
Stephen Mico, *Senior Vice President and Publisher,*
  Children's Books and Education Publishing Group

STAFF FOR THIS BOOK
Nancy Laties Feresten, *Vice President, Editor-in-Chief*
  of Children's Books
Suzanne Patrick Fonda, *Project Editor*
Robert D. Johnston, Ph.D., *Associate Professor and Director,*
  Teaching of History Program University of Illinois at Chicago,
  Series Editor
Bea Jackson, *Design Director, Children's Books and Education*
  Publishing Group
Margaret Sidlosky, *Illustrations Director*
Jim Hiscott, *Art Director*
Jean Cantu, *Illustrations Specialist*
Carl Mehler, *Director of Maps*
Justin Morrill and Martin S. Walz, *Map Research,*
  Design, and Production
Connie D. Binder, *Indexer*
Rebecca Hinds, *Managing Editor*
R. Gary Colbert, *Production Director*
Lewis R. Bassford, *Production Manager*
Vincent P. Ryan and Maryclare Tracy, *Manufacturing Managers*

Voices from Colonial Georgia was prepared by
CREATIVE MEDIA APPLICATIONS, INC.
Robin Doak, *Writer*
Fabia Wargin Design, Inc., *Design and Production*
Susan Madoff, *Editor*
Laurie Lieb, *Copyeditor*
Jennifer Bright, *Image Researcher*

Body text is set in Deepdene, sidebars are Caslon 337 Oldstyle, and display text is Cochin Archaic Bold.

LIBRARY OF CONGRESS CATALOGING-IN-PUBLICATION DATA
Doak, Robin S. (Robin Santos), 1963–
  Voices from colonial America. Georgia, 1521–1776 / by Robin Doak.
    p. cm. — (Voices from colonial America)
  Includes bibliographical references and index.
  ISBN-10: 0-7922-6389-8, ISBN-13: 978-0-7922-6389-0 (Hardcover); ISBN-10: 0-7922-6858-X; ISBN-13: 978-0-7922-6858-1 (Library)
  1. Georgia—History—Colonial period, ca. 1600-1775—Juvenile literature. I. Title. II. Series.
  F289.D65 2006
  975.8'02—dc22

                                      2005022141

Printed in Belgium

CONTENTS

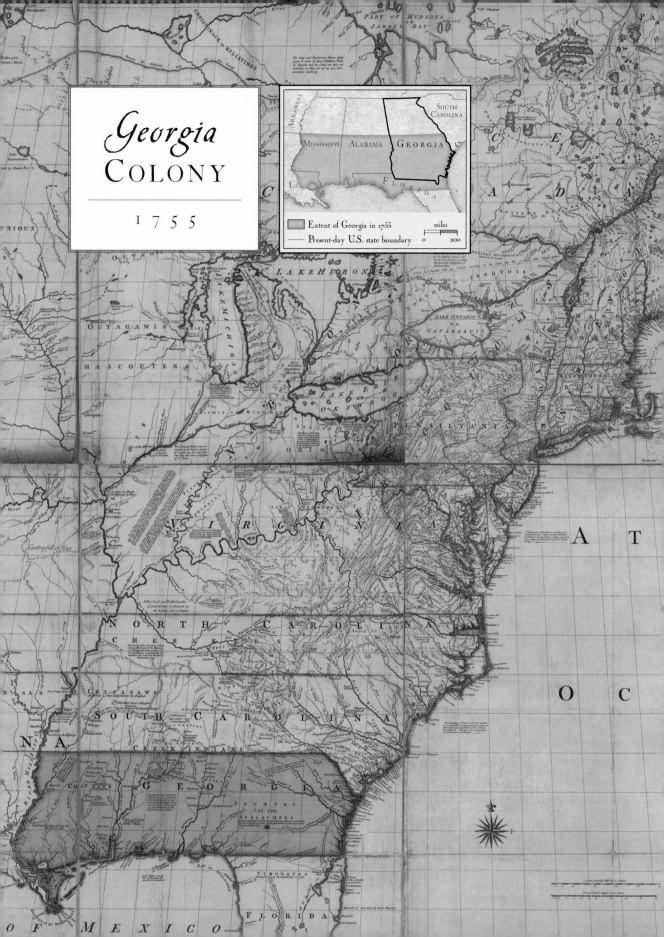

Georgia
COLONY

1755

SOUTH
CAROLINA

ARKANSAS

MISSISSIPPI ALABAMA GEORGIA

LA.

FLORIDA

Extent of Georgia in 1755

Present-day U.S. state boundary

miles

0   200

INTRODUCTION

by

Robert Olwell, Ph.D.

In 1734 James Oglethorpe took a group of Georgia Indians to England.
This painting is an artist's interpretation of their introduction to the
Trustees of the Georgia Colony.

Although Georgia is often described as the last of the British colonies along the East Coast of North America, the beginnings of its colonial history are older than any other state's except Florida's. Buried somewhere on St. Catherines Island are the traces of the first European effort to settle within what would one day become the United States.

OPPOSITE: John Mitchell's 1755 map has been colorized for this book to emphasize the boundaries of Georgia Colony according to its 1732 charter. The inset map shows present-day Georgia's boundaries for comparison.

From the establishment of the short-lived town of San Miguel de Gualdape to the Declaration of Independence, the colonial era of Georgia's history spanned exactly two hundred and fifty years.

For all but the last few decades of this era, the territory between the Savannah and St. Marys Rivers was a sparsely populated frontier region on which a variety of nations and peoples lived and fought. Over time, the names of these peoples changed from Guale, Ichisi, and Spanish to Yamassee and Creek, English and African.

For one hundred years, coastal Georgia was a mission province of Spanish Florida. After the destruction of the missions, the region became, for half a century, a no-man's land between the rival Spanish and British colonial empires. This lawless zone was a haven for pirates and other outcasts. Georgia acquired its present name in 1732 when it was organized as a philanthropic colony and named for the British king. Forty-four years later, Georgia patriots joined those in the 12 colonies to the north to declare independence from another King George. In 1788, Georgia was one of the first states to ratify the Constitution that transformed the 13 United States into a single nation.

The story of Georgia's colonial past is filled with many fascinating figures, each of whom contributed to making the state we know today. Hernando de Soto, a proud Spanish conquistador, traversed the region looking for the fabled cities of gold. Juanillo, a courageous Native American, led a revolt against the Spanish missions. James Oglethorpe, an English warrior turned philanthropist, dreamed of a colony where poor men could have a fresh start. Nathanael Greene, a "fighting Quaker" and George Washington's most trusted general, liberated Georgia from British rule at the end of the Revolutionary War.

Beside these famous men and women walked and struggled thousands of ordinary people who had ambitions and aspirations of their own. These ideas and dreams did not always agree, and the history of colonial Georgia and its eventual place in the new United States is a tale of conflict as well as of cooperation.

The first official seal of the Trustees of the Georgia Colony, which shows a silkworm, its cocoon, and a mulberry leaf, reflected the belief that the insect would thrive in Georgia's warm climate and provide Britain with the raw material to produce beautiful textiles.

CHAPTER ONE

The Spanish Era

THE SPANISH EXPLORE AND SETTLE GEORGIA, *but are soon driven out by English colonists to the north.*

eorgia was founded in 1732, making it the last of Britain's colonies along the Atlantic coast of what is now the United States to be settled. But the history of colonial Georgia actually began more than two centuries before British colonists arrived in Savannah, Georgia's first permanent town. In the early 1500s, Spanish slavers, settlers, and missionaries all left their mark on the land.

In 1525, the first Spaniards visited the area with a particular mission in mind: to enslave the native people in the region and take them to Spanish colonies in the Caribbean.

OPPOSITE: In the early 1500s Spanish conquistadors began to arrive in Georgia. Their main interest was in capturing Native Americans and forcing them to work in gold mines in Puerto Rico and other Spanish territories.

These Spanish slaving ships came from the island colony of Puerto Rico. Here, slaves were forced to mine for gold. The following year, a wealthy Spanish colonial official, slave trader, and adventurer from Santo Domingo, also known as Hispaniola (the island that contains present-day Haiti and the Dominican Republic), decided to found his own settlement in the New World. In September 1526, Lucas Vázquez de Ayllón and a group of about 600 colonists founded the Spanish settlement of San Miguel de Gualdape. In recent years historians and archaeologists have reread contemporary Spanish accounts of the settlement and believe that San Miguel de Gualdape was most likely located on St. Catherines Island off the coast of Georgia. The Spaniards called the coastal region of present-day Georgia Guale, the name that the native peoples of the area used.

colony—a settlement that is controlled by a distant country

archaeologist— someone who studies the people and customs of ancient times

San Miguel did not last long. The colonists argued among themselves over the settlement's leadership, and some of the settlement's African slaves rose up against their masters. The rebellion, combined with disease and starvation, led the remaining Spanish settlers to abandon the settlement after just six weeks and return to Santo Domingo.

In 1539–1540, Spanish conquistador Hernando de Soto financed his own expedition and set off to explore the southeastern

conquistador— a Spanish conqueror who explored the Americas in the 1500s

region of the present-day United States in search of gold, precious gems, and other valuables. De Soto and about 600 soldiers began their journey somewhere near Tampa, Florida, a region claimed by Juan Ponce de León for the Spanish in 1513. The party followed native pathways through Florida and into what is now southwest Georgia. During his journey, de Soto sought out the native people of the region and forced them to serve as guides and porters to carry equipment. His men stole food from the Indians, and left behind European diseases, such as smallpox and plague. These diseases would soon cause a serious decline in the native population.

smallpox—a contagious disease caused by a virus

plague—a deadly, contagious disease caused by bacteria

Hernando de Soto is credited with being the first European to discover the Mississippi River. Although this famous painting by William H. Powell shows the event as a triumphant occasion, in truth de Soto considered the river an obstacle to his quest for gold.

Hernando de Soto

Born in Spain around 1496, Hernando de Soto knew from an early age that he wanted to be a conquistador. As a teenager, de Soto and moved to Seville, hoping to find a place on a Spanish expedition of conquest. As a conquistador, he aided in the conquest of Peru. The riches that Spain gained there no doubt spurred his dreams of finding similar treasures in Florida. De Soto explored islands in the West Indies and Central and South America in what are now the countries of Panama, Nicaragua, and Colombia before setting out for Spanish Florida. De Soto also earned money as a slave trader.

On the North American mainland, de Soto and his men never found the treasure troves of gold that they believed were hidden somewhere in the Southeast region. However, he became the first European to discover the Mississippi River. In 1542, on the return journey, de Soto became sick and died in present-day Louisiana. His men buried him in the Mississippi. The rest of the party returned empty-handed to Mexico City the following year.

THE FIRST PEOPLE

Although the Spanish were the first Europeans in the Georgia area, other people had lived in the region for thousands of years.

Indians known as the Mississippian people arrived in Georgia around A.D. 800. These people settled together in small villages, growing food crops and hunting deer, turkeys, and other wild animals. Some tribes built huge mounds of earth that were used for burial sites, temples, and building platforms. The Creek, as the tribes de Soto met came to be known, were descendants of these earlier peoples. By 1600, diseases, contracted from early encounters with European explorers, had nearly destroyed the native populations.

By the early 1700s the Creek had become the dominant tribe in Georgia. The Creek were actually a loose confederation of several different tribes, each with its own language and traditions. These tribes included the Creek, Yamassee, Yamacraw, Savannah, and Westo. English traders were the first to call members of the confederation "Creek," a shortened version of *"Indians living on Ochese Creek."*

confederation—
an alliance of groups of
people with similar goals

The various Creek tribes lived in villages called *italwa*. Each *italwa* was governed by a *mico*. Micos were selected by the people of the village and could be replaced if they did a bad job.

mico—a Creek chief

The Creek were farming people. They grew corn, beans, squash, and sweet potatoes. They also hunted for deer and other small game in the forests surrounding their villages and caught fish and shellfish in nearby rivers. Deer meat was a source of protein in the Creek diet, while deerskins were used to make clothing.

Another important tribe in Georgia was the Cherokee. The Cherokee began moving into the area around 1450, forcing the Creek farther and farther south. Throughout the region's colonial history, the Cherokee and Creek fought for control of the northern part of Georgia.

The Cherokee, like the Creek, were farming people who lived in settled villages. However, the Cherokee spoke Iroquois, a different language from the one used by their Creek neighbors. The word "Cherokee" comes from the Creek word *chelokee*, which means "people of a different speech."

In the late 1700s, Chief Austenaco led the Cherokee Nation in a great war that forced the Creek out of present-day Georgia.

SPANISH MISSIONS

Not all early Spanish colonists were interested in finding gold and other riches in the New World. The goal of some Catholic settlers—and of Spain itself—was to spread Christianity throughout the Americas. Some of the first missionaries arrived in Georgia in 1568, but the Spanish mission period was strongest beginning in the late 1580s.

In 1595, a group of Franciscan monks founded six missions, each near one of the most important Indian villages. The missionaries expected to collect a *sabana* (tribute) of food from the Indians that they could use to feed themselves or export to St. Augustine, the capital of Spanish Florida. Some missionaries also recruited Indians to help them build their missions by imposing a *repartimiento*, or donation of labor, forcing the Indians to work a portion of their time in the fields or on construction projects. The priests relied on the Spanish soldiers provided by the government for protection. Once the building was completed, they went to work, holding Mass and teaching tribal children and adults about Catholicism.

In order to communicate with the Indians, the friars worked hard to learn the native languages, which they did with the help of interpreters. Some tribal chiefs, anxious for the trade goods and prestige that went with joining the mission system, asked missionaries to come to their villages.

The missionaries also wanted the Native Americans, whom they considered "savages," to adopt European lifestyles and culture. The missionaries urged the male Indians to have only one wife. They also encouraged the Indians to dress like Europeans and to stop roaming and set up permanent villages and farms. The Spaniards introduced European goods to the region, including livestock such as sheep and pigs. Over the next three years, the missionaries converted about 1,500 natives.

This engraving, from an account written by Spanish missionary Friar Pablo Beaumont, shows Native American women in European dress waiting to be baptized.

Some of the Native Americans resented the Spanish friars and resisted all efforts to convert them to Christianity. In 1597, a native Guale named Juanillo led a revolt that killed five missionaries and took one captive. A survivor later reported to the Spanish the speech that Juanillo made to his people after the attack:

> Now the friar is dead. This would not have happened if he had allowed us to live according to our pre-Christian manner. Let us return to our ancient customs. Let us provide for our defense against the punishment which the governor of Florida will mete out. . . . For he will punish us as severely for having killed one friar as if we had killed them all.

The uprising was eventually ended by troops sent by the Spanish governor of St. Augustine. Later, the Spanish would build presidios on the Sea Islands off the coast of Georgia. The main goal of Spanish troops stationed on the islands was to provide protection for the missionaries. In the coming years, the missionaries were more successful than ever in converting the natives to Christianity and European culture. The early 1600s became known as the golden age of the Spanish missions in Georgia.

presidio—a Spanish fortress

THE END OF THE MISSIONS

In 1670, English colonists founded South Carolina, just north of Guale. Soon after arriving, the English began stirring up trouble for the Spanish missionaries. Although the Spanish believed that Guale was their land, the English disagreed. Wanting to trade with the Indians of the region, they advanced their own claim to the land south of Carolina. One converted Indian woman reported that "*the English are united and confederated with another nation of thieving Indians . . . so that these make war on and disturb the natives already converted to the Catholic religion, ...*"

In the 1680s, hunters and traders from South Carolina began freely venturing into Guale. With the Westo tribe as their allies, the English raided the missions, forcing the Spanish to move to the Sea Islands off Georgia's coast. By

TENNESSEE
NORTH CAROLINA
<u>Cherokee</u>
SOUTH CAROLINA
Tennessee R.
<u>Muscogee</u>
Savannah R.
GEORGIA
<u>Yamasee</u>
Alabama R.
Ocmulgee R.
<u>Westo</u>
Chattahoochee R.
ALABAMA
<u>Savannah</u> □ *Santa Elena*
Altamaha R.
Santa Catalina □ — St. Catherines Is.
San Joseph de Sapala □ *San Miguel de Gualdape*
— *St. Simons Is.*
Guadalquini □
<u>Guale</u>
San Carlos □
San Nicolás
St. Marys R. — □ *San Pedro de Mocama*
□ *Santa Maria*
<u>Apalachee</u>
San Luis de Talimalí □
(Tallahassee)
<u>Timucua</u>
St. Augustine
Gulf of Mexico
FLORIDA

ATLANTIC OCEAN

Sea Islands

SPAIN'S SOUTHEASTERN EMPIRE IN NORTH AMERICA
<u>circa 1526-1660</u>

(Tampa) •

Spanish Claims circa 1660
CANADA
UNITED STATES
ATLANTIC OCEAN
GEORGIA
MEXICO
Gulf of Mexico
Santo Domingo
Cuba
PACIFIC OCEAN
Caribbean Sea
Hispañola
Puerto Rico
CENTRAL AMERICA
SOUTH AMERICA
☐ Claimed by Spain
Present-day boundaries shown

Claimed by Spain
Spanish Guale
Unexplored land
Route of De Soto
Present-day state boundary
□ Selected Spanish mission
<u>Creek</u> Indian tribe
<u>Muscogee</u> Indian language group
(Tampa) Present-day place-name
miles
0   50   100
Present-day shorelines shown

Hernando de Soto's quest for gold led to his discovery of the Mississippi River and strengthened Spain's claim to what is now the southeastern United States. Between 1526 and 1660 as many as 50 missions were established. They stretched north from St. Augustine to Santa Elena on the Atlantic and west to San Nicolás near the Gulf of Mexico.

1681, there were more than 600 adult Indians living in the 12 island missions. The largest was the mission of Guadalquini on St. Simons Island.

On the islands, the missionaries and converted natives became easy targets for pirates operating out of Charles Town (now Charleston), the capital of South Carolina. As early as 1660, the English had decided to do everything they could to force the Spanish out of the area below South Carolina. They hired seafaring robbers to wander the coastline, raiding and burning Spanish missions and attacking Spanish ships. In just three years, the number of missions dropped from 12 to 4, with the smaller missions banding together for better defense. The forts and the soldiers within were not strong enough to withstand the attacks of the pirates, and the missionaries could no longer look to St. Augustine for defense. The Spanish governor was busy using his small force of soldiers to deal with pirate raids on the territorial capital and other Spanish holdings in Florida.

By October 1684, the last Spanish missions in Guale were attacked and raided by English pirates. Two of the missions were burned, and by early 1685, the remaining missionaries and their converts moved beyond the St. Marys River into Spanish Florida. Converts captured by the pirates were sold as slaves to work in the West Indies. Although the Spanish no longer had a presence in the region that would someday be called Georgia, they would continue to cling to their claim to the coastal territory they knew as Guale.

CHAPTER TWO

A Buffer Colony

THE ENGLISH DECIDE TO SETTLE GEORGIA *as a "buffer colony" between South Carolina and Florida, and one man is willing to do the job.*

nglish colonists in South Carolina had succeeded in driving the Spanish into Florida. After the last missions in Georgia were destroyed, however, the Spaniards launched a raid into South Carolina in 1686 to take revenge. Although the raid failed, it was a warning to the English colonists: Carolinians needed something between them and the Spanish.

To protect themselves from future Spanish raids, Carolina colonists constructed Fort King George in 1721.

OPPOSITE: Captain Edward Teach, better known as the pirate Blackbeard, preyed on merchant ships in the Caribbean Sea and along the southeastern coast of what is now the United States.

Located on the Altamaha River, the fort served as a very visible warning. It included a blockhouse, soldiers' quarters, and a guardhouse that was also used as a hospital. Fort King George, which was never attacked by the Spanish, was abandoned in 1727 after it fell into disrepair.

blockhouse—a small fortress made of timber or logs

Carolinians knew they needed a permanent answer to their Spanish problem. The perfect solution would be a British "buffer colony" between Carolina and Florida. Settling the region would also make Britain's claim to the region stronger than Spain's claim. An added benefit of settlement in the region to the

buffer colony—a colony between two larger colonies controlled by different countries

south would be that native people would be forced out of the area. Like the Spanish before them, the British colonists wanted the native lands for their own, where colonists could settle free from attack and trouble.

PIRATES ON THE GEORGIA COAST

In the early 1700s, Georgia's status as an unclaimed no-man's-land lured pirates to its coast. With its swamps, marshes, islands, and creeks, the region was a perfect hideout for the pirates' illegal activities. Two of the most famous coastal raiders were Edward Teach, better known as Blackbeard, and Stede Bonnet, the "gentleman pirate."

Under cover of darkness, pirates (in the small vessel) approach a large Spanish ship in hopes of stealing gold, weapons, and other valuable cargo.

Born in either England or the island of Jamaica in the West Indies, Teach began his pirate career by raiding Spanish ships off the coasts of Georgia and Florida. One of the most notorious men of his time, Blackbeard sailed the ocean in the *Queen Anne's Revenge*. To show how fearless he was, Teach would place slow-burning pieces of rope in his hair and his long black beard and light them on fire.

According to legend, Bonnet was a former British Army officer and Barbados plantation owner who took to piracy to escape a nagging wife. Eventually, he and Blackbeard banded together against the British colonists.

The colonists had originally welcomed— and even encouraged—pirate raids on Spanish ships and settlements. Pirates who took part in "legal" attacks against enemy ships were known as privateers. Privateers owned their

privateer—a pirate hired by a government to attack and rob the ships of enemy countries

own ships and were licensed by the British government to prey upon enemy ships. They could keep whatever they captured or sell it for a profit. The pirates boosted colonial economies by selling their booty and spending their money in colonial ports. The pirates also scared off French and Spanish attackers.

The age of privateering ended in 1713. That year, the Treaty of Utrecht established peaceful relations between Great Britain, Spain, and France. However, many privateers refused to give up their old ways. Pirates like Blackbeard and Bonnet raised a new flag—the skull and crossbones—and began attacking British ships. In 1717, Blackbeard even blockaded Charles Town and held some of its citizens ransom. The colonists in Virginia and the Carolinas demanded that the British government put an end to the pirates' raids. In June 1718, Blackbeard died while battling the British Navy off the coast of North Carolina. Six months later, Bonnet's career came to an end on the gallows in Charles Town. In 1996 divers discovered what may be the wreck of the *Queen Anne's Revenge*.

gallows—a wooden structure used for hanging people

JAMES OGLETHORPE'S NOBLE EXPERIMENT

Back in Great Britain, one man was formulating a plan for a new settlement. James Oglethorpe, a member of Britain's

Parliament—
Great Britain's lawmaking body

Parliament, wanted to create a colony for people in need of a second chance, the *"useless poor in England and distressed Protestants in Europe."* (At this time, the state religion in Britain was the Church of England, a branch of Protestantism. However, other Protestant groups in England who didn't follow the teachings of the state church could be persecuted.) Oglethorpe had long been concerned about the plight of the poor and the imprisoned in Britain. Not only had he spent time in jail, but a close friend had died of neglect while in debtor's prison. In Britain at this time, people who owed money were thrown in jail without a trial and with little hope of being able to pay their debt and thus be released from prison.

debtor's prison—
a prison for people who owe money but cannot repay their debts

Oglethorpe and his friend John Perceval, the Earl of Egmont, focused their hopes on settling the territory south of South Carolina. By founding a settlement here, they believed they would give Britain a strong presence in the so-called no-man's-land now claimed by both the British colonists to the north and the Spanish to the south.

A group of convicts in chains gets ready to board a ship that will take them from England to Georgia, where they would be given a chance to make a fresh start. In truth, very few of the people who settled in Oglethorpe's colony were freed prisoners.

In April 1732, Oglethorpe, Perceval, and 19 friends and associates received a 21-year charter from King George II for the colony of Georgia, to be located south of South Carolina. These trustees chose the colony's name as a way to honor King George. The Trustees were responsible for governing and overseeing the welfare of the new colony. The king, however, was not particularly interested in Oglethorpe's plan to aid the poor. Of greater importance was the fact that this new colony would provide the much-needed buffer between British colonies and Spanish Florida and help prevent future attacks by hostile natives. The charter issued to Oglethorpe and the other Trustees laid out King George's concerns:

charter—a document that grants a colony the right to exist

Trustees—the 21 men chosen to run the colony of Georgia

> Our Provinces in North America have been frequently Ravaged by Indian Enemies, more especially that of South Carolina, which in the late war by the neighboring Savages was laid wast [waste] with Fire and Sword and great numbers of English Inhabitants miserably Massacred, and our Loving Subjects who now Inhabit these by reason of the Smallness of their numbers will in case of any new war be Exposed to the like Calamities in as much as their whole Southern Frontier continueth unsettled and lieth open.

PREPARING TO MIGRATE

After receiving the royal charter, the Trustees in Britain began working toward their goal of creating a hardworking society of small farmers that could provide trade goods to Britain. They believed that colonists in Georgia would thrive by producing silk and wine, items that could not be produced in Britain and were expensive for the British to purchase from other countries. According to reports, the climate and land of Georgia made it an ideal place for producing such items. *In Rationale for Founding the Georgia Colony,* Oglethorpe wrote, *"By such a Colony, many families, who would otherwise starve, will be provided for, and made masters of houses and lands."*

James Edward Oglethorpe
1696–1785

To encourage poor British people to migrate to Georgia, the Trustees offered 50 acres (20 ha) and free passage to the new colony. The Trustees tried to lure those who weren't poor, too. Those who paid for their own voyage to the New World—and brought ten of their own white servants with them—would be given up to 500 acres. First, however, those hoping to migrate to Georgia had to be interviewed by the Trustees: Only people who deserved a second chance and seemed willing to work hard were to be allowed to settle in the new colony. Although the Trustees hoped to send about 100 families to Georgia, they had difficulty finding "worthy poor." In December 1732, Lord Egmont wrote, "*We examined about thirty poor people who applied to go over. . . . Most of them we rejected. . . .*"

The Trustees also looked for carpenters, farmers, bakers, tailors, and others who they felt would help Georgia grow. And they encouraged whole families to migrate, "*for a wife and children are security of a man's not abandoning the settlement and the presence of those dear pledges . . . will the more strongly incite him to labor.*"

As a result, the number of imprisoned poor people who migrated to Georgia was quite small. Of the first 100 settlers, very few were people released from debtor's prison. Many people in Britain eagerly embraced Oglethorpe's "Great Experiment," as he called it. Anglican ministers preached about the benefits of Georgia. Church groups collected money to help pay for the new

Anglican—a member of the Church of England

colony, and Parliament even agreed to send money each year to help Georgia's colonists survive. Like Oglethorpe, Parliament may have been thinking of the success of William Penn's colony, Pennsylvania. In 1733, Oglethorpe wrote, "*Within this 50 years, Pennsylvania was as much a forest as Georgia is now; and in these few years, by the wise economy of William Penn, and those who assisted him, it now gives food to 80,000 inhabitants, and can boast of as fine a City as most in Europe.*"

The MARGRAVATE *of* AZILIA

ONE OF THE FIRST PEOPLE TO PROPOSE settling the Georgia area was a Scot named Sir Robert Montgomery. In 1717, he was granted land between the Savannah and Altamaha Rivers by the proprietors of Carolina. The baron intended to call his new settlement the Margravate of Azilia. A margravate is a historic German territory ruled by a prince or military governor. Historians are not sure why Montgomery chose the name "Azilia." To encourage settlement, Montgomery published a description of the region, calling it *"the most amiable Country of the Universe: that Nature has not bless'd the World with any Tract, which can be preferable to it; that Paradise with all her Virgin Beauties, may be modestly suppos'd at most but equal to its Native Excellencies."* Montgomery was not able to find enough people willing to settle the region within three years, however, and his land grant was voided.

James Oglethorpe was happy to sign on as one of Georgia's first settlers. The rest of the Trustees, however, would stay in Britain and govern their colony from afar. Oglethorpe, the only "resident Trustee," was given leadership powers. However, the royal charter prevented him from holding any official title, owning any land, or receiving a salary from the colonists. After all, the Trustees had taken as their motto the Latin phrase *Non sibi sed aliis,* or "not for self, but for others." Oglethorpe was quick to mortgage his property in Britain to help finance the new colony. ❈

CHAPTER THREE

A Noble Experiment

1733 – 1738

ENGLISHMAN JAMES OGLETHORPE *founds Savannah,*
Georgia's first settlement, and early colonists
struggle for survival.

n November 17, 1732, the ship *Anne* set out from London. On board were 114 settlers bound for the new colony of Georgia. Included on the ship's passenger list were Oglethorpe, several carpenters, a gardener, a surgeon, a miller, a baker, two wigmakers, a stocking maker, and many others.

OPPOSITE: This 19th-century engraving shows James Oglethorpe's first meeting with the Yamacraw people near present-day Savannah in early 1733. He formed a life-long friendship with their chief, Tomochichi.

According to the lease between the *Anne's* captain and the Trustees, the travelers were promised *"four beef days, two pork days and one fish day every week during being on their passage."* The captain was also required to stock water, beer, bread, peas, butter, and plums.

On January 13, 1733, after nearly two months at sea, the *Anne* weighed anchor at Charles Town, South Carolina. While the colonists remained behind in South Carolina, Oglethorpe and a few others went ahead by boat to Georgia to choose a good spot for the first town. He selected Yamacraw Bluff, on the **bluff**—a high cliff along a river Savannah River. Oglethorpe believed that the site would be easy to defend and safe from river flooding. Then, as today, the Savannah River served as the boundary between South Carolina and Georgia.

When Oglethorpe reported to the Trustees about his choice, he wrote,

> *I went myself to view the Savannah River. I fixed upon a healthy situation about ten miles from the sea. The river here forms a half moon, along the South side of which the banks are almost forty foot [12 m] high and on top flat, which they call a bluff. Ships that draw twelve foot [3.7 m] water can ride within ten yards [9 m] of the bank. Upon the river side in the center of this plain, I have laid out the town.*

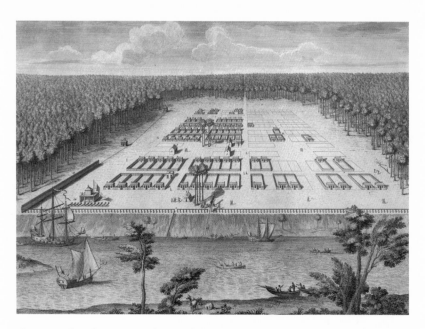

The city plan for Savannah was based on a repeated pattern of neighborhoods, or wards, with wide streets, public parks, and town squares for businesses. Oglethorpe supervised construction from his tent at the edge of the bluff (front, center).

HOME IN SAVANNAH

In early February, the first Georgia colonists arrived at their new home. Oglethorpe had prepared for the colonists by having wooden steps built so the new arrivals could easily climb to the top of the steep cliff.

The settlers' first task was to set up the five large tents that would serve as their homes for more than a month. The next item of business was to build a 14-foot (4-m)-tall palisade fence around the settlement to protect it from attack. Later, the colonists set to work building the first wooden houses.

palisade—a fence made out of wooden stakes

Oglethorpe had sketched out a plan for Georgia's first settlement in February, after selecting the Yamacraw Bluff site. The town was originally divided into four wards. A ward consisted of several building sites organ-ized around a central, open square. Each ward had its own name and its own constable to make sure things ran smoothly. Streets connected the wards to one another. In time, the number of wards in Savannah would grow to 28, with all but four having the same basic layout as those planned by Oglethorpe.

ward—a section of a city or settlement

One of the first projects in Savannah was the public garden. The garden was an experiment to see what would grow in Georgia's temperate climate. Cuttings were brought from the West Indies and South America to plant in the ten-acre (4-ha) garden. Many different types of trees, including orange, mulberry, and bamboo were planted. Olives, figs, and tea were also grown in the garden. Another early project was the building of a large, hand-cranked crane used to hoist supplies to the top of Yamacraw Bluff. Colonists built a public jail, dug a well, and built an oven, where people could bring their bread and other goods to bake.

STAKING A BRITISH CLAIM

To discourage Spanish attacks on the new Georgia colony, Ogelthorpe erected several forts along Georgia's coastline between 1733 and 1736. The most southerly fort was located on St. Marys River, the border between Georgia and the Spanish colony of Florida. The most important fortress in Georgia was Fort Frederica on St. Simons Island. Built in 1735, the fort was made of wood and sod. A town, called Frederica, soon grew up around the fort. At first, settlers built tent-like structures using palmetto leaves rather than canvas as the covering. Later, they built more permanent homes.

palmetto—a small palm tree with fan-shaped leaves

An Early View of SAVANNAH

A BRITISH COLONIST NAMED FRANCIS MOORE ARRIVED IN Georgia in 1736 to help settle Frederica, a town on St. Simons Island. Moore had been appointed keeper of the stores (supplies) of the new settlement and later served as the town recorder. In an account of his experiences, he later recalled his first glimpse of Savannah:

The town of Savannah is built of wood. . . . Their houses are built at a pretty large distance from one another for fear of fire. The streets are very wide, and there are great squares left at proper distances for markets and other conveniences. Near the river side is a guard house enclosed with palisades a foot (0.3 m) thick, where there are nineteen or twenty cannons mounted and a continual guard kept.

NEW NEIGHBORS

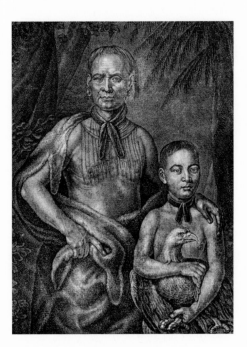

Yamacraw chief Tomochichi (circa 1642–1739) and his nephew Tooanahowi

Oglethorpe wanted to build good relations with the Native Americans in Georgia. In May 1733, he signed a treaty with a number of Creek chiefs. Oglethorpe encouraged the Trustees to pass laws aimed at regulating trade with the Native Americans and protecting them from being taken advantage of by some Carolina traders.

Thanks to Oglethorpe's decent treatment of the Indians, Savannah's early settlers could rely on help from the Native Americans in the region. One Indian who helped the settlers was a Creek woman named Coosaponakeesa. As the wife of an honest white trader from South Carolina, she was known to the colonists as Mary Musgrove. Musgrove aided peaceful relations between Indians and whites by acting as an interpreter for James Oglethorpe. In 1761, her third husband described Musgrove's important role:

> Nor would [the native people] have permitted Mr. Oglethorpe
> & his people a Quiet Possession . . . had not the Governor &

Council wrote to Mrs. [Musgrove] . . . to use the utmost of her Interest with the Indians for that Purpose and to give the new settlers all the Aid & Assistance their Necessities might require. . . .

Despite the good start, problems between the Indians and the white settlers would soon arise. The Indians did not have the same concept of land ownership that the new arrivals had. When the Indians accepted gifts and payment for land, they believed that they were being paid for permission to live and hunt on the land. They expected to be able to still live and hunt on the same land themselves. Under the European concept of land ownership, the Indians no longer had the right to use the land. In the years to come, the Creek began calling Georgia colonists *Ecunnaunuxulgee*, or "people greedily grasping after the lands of [the native] people."

A Hearty Welcome

IN MARCH 1733, COLONIST Thomas Causton described the Georgia settlers' first meeting with the Native Americans of the area:

At our first landing, they came to bid us welcome, and before them came a man dancing in antic postures with a spread fan of white feathers in each hand as a token of friendship, which were fixed to small rods about four foot (1. 2 m) long, set from top to bottom with small bells . . . which made a jingling, whilst the king and others followed making a very uncouth hollering. . . .

KEEPING ORDER

Savannah's acknowledged leader was James Oglethorpe, who himself reported to the Trustees back in London. All legal changes and problems had to be written down and mailed across the Atlantic Ocean to be handled there.

One of Georgia's early laws banned lawyers, a profession known then as the *"pest and scourge of mankind."* As a result, people accused of a crime were forced to defend themselves. Those found guilty of minor crimes, such as drunkenness, were put in the stocks. More serious crimes were punished with whippings and deportation from the new colony. Another early law banned hard liquor in the colony. The Trustees thought that alcohol would make their colonists ill and lazy.

People guilty of minor crimes were often sentenced
to spend time with their feet, hands, or head
stuck through holes in a wooden structure called a stock.

Georgia was also the only colony to ban slavery within its limits. The Trustees were afraid that the presence of African slaves would make Europeans afraid to migrate to the colony, for fear that the slaves would rebel. The Trustees also wanted to instill a strong work ethic (a set of values based on belief in hard work and self-discipline) in the Georgia colonists by requiring them to do their own labor.

SURVIVING IN A NEW COLONY

By September 1733, more people had arrived in Savannah from Britain, bringing the total number of colonists to about 400. Men farmed, hunted, and traded to survive. Because Britain was counting on the colony to produce silk, the colonists were expected to plant 100 mulberry trees on every 10 acres (4 ha) of land. Mulberry trees served as food for the silkworms that Britain imported from China. Unfortunately, the silk industry never amounted to anything, and the colonists eventually abandoned their efforts.

Women planted kitchen gardens and raised poultry to feed their families. They took care of their homes and raised their children. Any clothing that their family needed was sewed or knitted by the women of the house.

By the first summer, the Savannah colonists had tired of their strange new environment. The swampy land was a breeding ground for life-threatening pests such as alligators, rattlesnakes, and mosquitos that carried malaria. The weather was not what the settlers had been led to expect. The summer was much hotter and the winter much colder.

malaria—a disease spread by the bite of infected mosquitoes

The constant hard labor also took a toll. Some of the earliest colonists had been unable to earn a living back in Britain but who were not suited to life on the frontier. Many of these settlers fled to the more economically developed colony of South Carolina. Those who stayed behind quickly began to blame Oglethorpe and the Trustee system for their problems.

OTHER GROUPS ARRIVE

While planning his "Noble Experiment," Oglethorpe had actively recruited groups of persecuted Protestants from other lands in Europe to settle in Georgia. One such group was from Salzburg, a German-speaking region between Austria and Bavaria. The Salzburgers were Lutherans, Protestants who followed the teachings of Martin Luther. Luther was a former Catholic priest who had split with the church in 1520. In the early 1700s, the Lutherans in Salzburg were exiled by Catholic officials there.

In March 1734, 78 Salzburgers arrived in Georgia. They founded their own settlement, called Ebenezer, 25 miles (40 km) upriver from Savannah. During Georgia's colonial period, Ebenezer was a center for German-speaking immigrants, where they could feel at home and live near others who shared a similar culture. By the 1770s, an estimated 1,200 Germans had migrated to Georgia.

The Salzburgers, Protestant refugees from present-day Austria and Bavaria, a region in Germany, prepare to leave for Georgia.

The industrious Salzburgers planted crops and built homes, a gristmill, and a sawmill. They established the first orphanage in the American colonies. Within five years, the settlement was thriving, and the new colonists were asking the Trustees to send their friends and family members to Georgia:

*We have with one accord wrote a letter . . . and in that letter
expressly named those Salzburgers and Austrians who as our
friends, relations and countrymen we wish to see settled here.
. . . We have given them an account of our being settled well
and being mighty well pleased with the climate and condition
of this country.*

Savannah's JEWISH POPULATION

IN JULY 1733, A GROUP OF 42 JEWISH PEOPLE ARRIVED in Savannah from London. Jews, along with Roman Catholics, were among the few peoples not wanted by the Trustees. For centuries, Jewish people had suffered prejudice and discrimination around the globe because of their religion. Because Great Britain's traditional enemies, France and Spain, were Catholic countries, all Catholics were viewed with suspicion. However, the Jews were allowed to remain in the colony. One of the new arrivals was a physician who treated the colonists suffering from disease, and Oglethorpe felt he might play a useful and important role.

The first Jewish colonists were refugees, fleeing religious persecution. Most were originally from Portugal and spoke no English; instead, they spoke Portuguese, Spanish or German. Although some left the colony and moved to South Carolina, others chose to remain. They founded Congregation Mickve Israel, the third oldest Jewish congregation in the United States.

In 1735, a group of immigrants from the Scottish Highlands (in northern Scotland) arrived in Georgia. The new arrivals, recruited from their native land to protect the colony's border with Spain, founded the town of New Inverness, later renamed Darien, on the Altamaha River. Soon, groups of Lowland Scots from the southeast part of Scotland also arrived, settling Josephs Town a few miles from Savannah. Later, many Scots moved to Savannah. There, the

Scottish Highlanders who settled in Georgia did double duty as farmers and defenders of the frontier against possible attack from Spanish Florida.

Scots earned money by renting out the servants they had brought from Scotland. In 1736, groups of Irish, Welsh, Dutch, and Moravian immigrants also moved to Georgia.

In 1736, British colonists settled the town of Augusta. Augusta had been founded as a Carolina trading post called Fort Moore. Later, Georgia colonists settled near the fort, naming their new town "Augusta" after the Princess of Wales (and future mother of King George III). After a visit in 1739, James Oglethorpe described Augusta as *of great service . . . and the Key of all the Indian Countrey*" because it linked Georgia's colonists with the vast, unsettled frontier to the west. Located at the source of the Savannah River, the town was a vital center for trade with the Native Americans of the region. ▦

CHAPTER FOUR

A Colony at War

1739 — 1748

GEORGIA BECOMES A BATTLEGROUND *in the ongoing conflict between England and Spain.*

hrough most of the 1730s, Britain and Spain tried to peacefully resolve their struggles over the "debatable land," as the British called Georgia. When those efforts failed, both countries took to other tactics to rid themselves of their unwanted neighbors. Both the Spanish and the British tried to ally themselves with the Indian tribes of the region by giving them food, weapons, and other gifts.

OPPOSITE: This cartoon showing Britain's prime minister (seated) almost fainting at the sight of Robert Jenkins's pickled ear (it had been cut off seven years before by a Spanish commander) rekindled British anger over the incident and led to a war with Spain.

This 1741 map shows the cities, forts, and roads of Oglethorpe's Georgia in relation to Charleston (Charles Town) and St. Augustine. The inset map shows St. Simons Island (Great St. Simon's), Fort Frederica, and the sound that separates St. Simons from Jekyll (Jekyl) Island. A note on the main map confirms that the water here is deep enough for the safe passage of 40 gun ships.

In the late 1730s, the Spanish ratcheted up their attempts to cause trouble in Georgia. In a letter to the Trustees written in October 1738, Oglethorpe reported, *"The Spaniards have tempted the Creek Indians with great presents to join against us, which they have refused. . . . The Spaniards reported that I had been disgraced in England and that I should never return. . . . I shall see [the Creek] in a few days at Savannah. This will be a new expense, for there must be presents given to them."*

At the same time, Oglethorpe also worried about keeping control in his own colony, especially over the rebellious British troops that had been sent from Britain in 1736 and 1737 to defend Georgia from the Spanish. In November 1738, Oglethorpe, now a brevet (temporary) general of all the British forces in Georgia and Carolina, faced a mutiny of soldiers at Fort St. Andrews on Cumberland Island, north of the St. Marys River. The soldiers were upset that they hadn't been paid in months. Although he managed to end the mutiny, Oglethorpe was nearly hit by a bullet that came so close that his clothes were singed.

THE WAR OF JENKINS'S EAR

In October 1739, the problems between Spain and Britain finally erupted into full-scale warfare. The conflict, known as the War of Jenkins's Ear, was named after an incident that had occurred eight years earlier in 1731, when the crew of a Spanish privateer cut off the ear of a British captain named Robert Jenkins. When the incident resurfaced in 1738, Jenkins was asked to give testimony in court. It caused such outrage in Britain that all the efforts at diplomacy during the previous years failed.

In the American colonies, only Georgia was truly affected by the war. The Spanish wanted "their" territory back, and the newest British colony's very existence was at stake. The high stakes for Georgia were driven home forcefully when Spanish troops attacked nearby Amelia Island, off the coast of northeastern Florida, in November 1739. Two British men were killed during the attack. According to Oglethorpe, the men were decapitated, their bodies then *"mangled . . . most barbarously."* He pledged to the Trustees to *"die hard and . . . not lose one inch of ground without fighting."*

In retaliation for the assault on Amelia Island, Oglethorpe and a force of 900 British troops and 1,100 Indians marched into Florida in January 1740. The Georgians attacked two forts west of St. Augustine, burning Fort Picolata and capturing Fort Saint Francis de Pupa.

In May, Oglethorpe laid siege to St. Augustine itself. The general had planned to attack sooner, but had been forced to wait for reinforcements from South Carolina. By the time they arrived, the Spanish in St. Augustine had been able to stock up on supplies and fresh troops. As a result, Oglethorpe's spring siege failed, and he returned to Georgia in August, a sick man. In January 1741, he wrote to a friend, *"I cannot but say that other people's not acting with the* same vigour as I expected for the public service might contribute much to my sickness, but my illness never hindered me from being present at every place necessary either by land or by water."

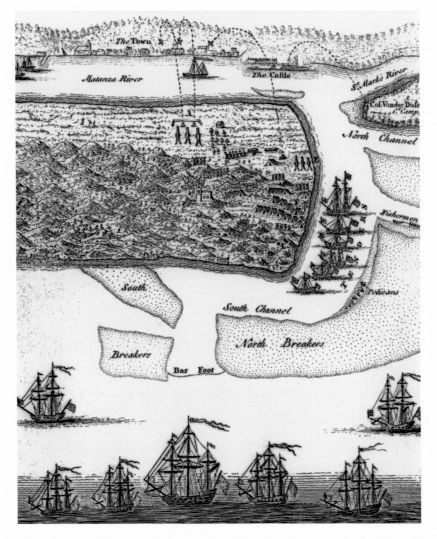

This drawing shows Oglethorpe's attack on St. Augustine ("The Town") from Eustatia Island during the War of Jenkins's Ear. The seven British ships in the foreground landed troops on the near side of the island then blocked the channel to the right of the island. Oglethorpe set up camp along the channel. His men can be seen moving cannon into position on the far side of the island. The dashed lines indicate missile fire.

In June 1742, the Spanish launched a massive sea invasion of Georgia, sending 51 ships from Cuba to attack the colony. The Spaniards hoped to capture Georgia easily, then move north and take control of South Carolina. Things didn't quite work as planned, however. In July, as many as 5,000 Spaniards came up against Oglethorpe's soldiers and their Native American allies at Bloody Marsh on St. Simons Island, just 1 mile (1.6 km) from Fort Frederica. The Georgia troops, which numbered less than 1,000, were victorious, attacking the Spanish from behind the heavy trees and brush of the swampy area. Confused by the smoke and gunfire, the Spanish were forced to retreat. It was the last time that Spain would try to attack and capture Georgia.

In a letter to the Duke of Newcastle, Oglethorpe had this to say about his victory:

> Having intelligence from the Spanish camp that they had lost four captains and upwards of 200 men in the last action, besides a great many killed in the sea fight and several killed in the night by the Indians even within or near the camp, and that they had held a council of war in which there were great divisions . . . and that there was a general terror amongst them.

Despite the victory, the preparations for battle took a heavy toll on Georgia's citizens. Men in the fledgling colony were forced to turn their attentions to war, and the economy suffered. The residents of Savannah, in a state of near-constant panic, neglected their fields in order to build a fort for defense. At one point, the women and children of the town were evacuated.

A view of the port of Savannah, which was protected by several forts and British ships patrolling the harbor

FORT FREDERICA

Fort Frederica, located on St. Simons Island, became especially important during the period leading up to and during the War of Jenkins's Ear. The fort itself was made out of tabby, a cement-like mixture of lime, seashells, and sand. It was defended by a number of 18-pound (8-k) guns.

lime—a solid white substance sometimes created by burning shells or bones

The town of Frederica lay outside the fortress walls, but was protected by a wall of its own. In 1745, an *"anonymous young gentleman"* described the town:

The town is divided into several spacious streets, along whose sides are planted orange trees which in some time will have a very pretty effect on the view and will render the town pleasingly shady. . . . Some houses are built entirely of brick, some of brick and wood, some few of tabby-work, but most of the meaner sort of wood only. . . .

They have a market every day. The inhabitants of the town may be divided into officers, merchants, storekeepers, artisans and people in the provincial service. And there are often also many sojourners from the neighboring settlements and from New York, Philadelphia and Carolina on account of trade.

Oglethorpe himself spent time at the fort. In November 1738, he wrote sarcastically to a friend,

I am here in one of the most delightful situations as any man could wish to be: a great number of debts, empty magazines, no money to supply them, numbers of people to be fed, mutinous soldiers to command, a Spanish claim and a large body of their troops not far from us. But . . . these difficulties . . . rather animate than daunt me.

Fort Frederica CUISINE

LIFE FOR A SOLDIER AT FORT Frederica was not easy. The men often had to rely for food on whatever they could catch. One young man who served in Oglethorpe's troops described the meals:

The 'possum . . . eats [tastes] like a pig and is very nourishing. The raccoon is delicate eating, somewhat tasted like lamb. Squirrels are also most delicious food.

SETTLING THE DEBATE

Encouraged by the victory at Bloody Marsh, Oglethorpe again attacked St. Augustine in March 1743. Once again, the attack was not successful. Oglethorpe and his men returned to Georgia. The assault was the last armed conflict of the war on the American mainland. In Europe, the war merged into a larger conflict, called the War of Austrian Succession, which pitted Great Britain and Austria against France and Spain. The focus of fighting between Britain and Spain shifted away from America to Europe.

In 1748, Spain and Great Britain signed a peace treaty that officially ended the wars between them. Under the terms of the treaty, the two nations agreed that all colonial territories would be returned to their previous owners and that the St. Johns River would serve as the border between British Georgia and Spanish Florida.

The town of Frederica was one of the few settlements in Georgia to suffer as a direct result of the war's end. With the Spanish no longer a threat, the fortress in Frederica was abandoned. When the soldiers left, the town's economy suffered, and it soon fell into ruin. By 1755, a Georgia official reported that *"the fortifications were entirely decayed, and the houses falling down."* ✳

CHAPTER FIVE

The Experiment Fails

1738 — 1751

UNHAPPY COLONISTS FORCE *an end to Oglethorpe's "Noble Experiment," as the Trustees give up on Georgia.*

 eorgia's success as a Trustee colony was hampered by both the war with Spain and the unrealistic expectations of some colonists. From 1737 to 1741, the population of Georgia is thought to have decreased from 5,000 to 500.

OPPOSITE: George Whitefield, a central figure in the religious movement known as the Great Awakening, came to Georgia at the urging of missionary friends in 1738 and preached to crowds that gathered in open areas to hear him.

An early colonist, Phillip Thicknesse, complained, "*The truth was that I had been so poisoned by the glaring colors in which Oglethorpe had in his printed books displayed the prospects of his new colony of Georgia.*" Oglethorpe's letters home to the Trustees were filled with constant requests for more: more money, more supplies, and more settlers. He was quick to blame the quality of Savannah's colonists for their failure. In 1739, he wrote to the Trustees, comparing the Scottish settlers of Darien to the British in Savannah: "*The Darien hath been one of the settlements where the people have been most industrious, as those at Savannah have been most idle.*" Even Darien, with its hardworking Scots, struggled to thrive. By 1741, only 80 people remained in the town, less than half of the 166 Scots who had settled the town in 1735.

To see what life could be like in the New World, all Georgians had to do was look at their neighbors to the north in South Carolina. Here, residents owned their own land without the restrictions that Georgia colonists had. South Carolina colonists also owned slaves who performed all the hard work. To the eyes of

POOR AS A *Georgian*

COLONIAL GEORGIA QUICKLY gained a reputation among the other colonies as being a miserable place to live. In 1740, a colonist named Henry Garrett wrote, "*I got into a very bad corner of the world, where poverty and oppression abound to such a degree that it's become proverbial this way to say 'as poor as a Georgian.'*"

Georgia's residents, their neighbors to the north lived in comfort and ease. It didn't take long for Georgia colonists to start demanding the same rights allowed to residents of South Carolina.

One right that Georgia's colonists wanted was the right to leave their land to whomever they chose—including wives and daughters. Under the Trustees' rules, colonists could leave land and property only to an eldest son. The Trustees did not want women owning property that could otherwise be held by a man fit for military service and other duties.

What Georgians most wanted, however, was to be allowed to own slaves. Colonists were convinced that Georgia would never prosper until the Trustees lifted the ban on slavery. They saw their neighbors in South Carolina prospering under a plantation system. They wanted to follow suit.

plantation—a large self-sufficient farm

petition—a written request or plea to a person or group in power, usually signed by a number of people

In December 1738, 121 unhappy colonists sent a petition to the Trustees in Britain. The first part of the petition outlined the colonists' inability to flourish in Georgia:

The settlers here, they must unavoidably have access to and depend upon trade. . . . It is very well known that Carolina can raise everything that this colony can and they, having their labour so much cheaper, will always ruin our market unless we are in some measure on a footing with them.

In this hand-colored woodcut slaves unload rice barges along a river. Rice, Georgia's first staple crop became its most important commodity once slavery was finally allowed in the colony in 1751.

The second part of the petition set forth the colonists' suggestion for a "remedy" for their problems: *"the use of Negroes with proper limitations, which if granted would both induce great numbers of white people to come here and also render us capable to subsist ourselves by raising provisions upon our lands."*

Despite the petition, the Trustees continued the ban on slavery in Georgia. They had the support of some of Georgia's residents, including the Salzburgers and the Highland Scots in Darien. The Salzburgers, however, did not oppose slavery out of concern for human rights. In March 1739, they wrote to James Oglethorpe, *"We humbly beseech the Honourable Trustees not to allow it that any Negro might be brought to our place or in our neighbourhood, knowing by experience that houses and gardens will be robbed always by them and white people are in danger of life because of them, besides other great inconveniences."*

Although the original arguments against slavery had more to do with the welfare of the colony and white colonists, a few settlers were concerned about the morality of enslaving another people. Oglethorpe himself wrote to the Trustees that slavery would *"occasion the misery of thousands in Africa . . . who now live free there."*

THE RISE OF THE MALCONTENTS

The colonists who wanted to change the laws made by the Trustees came to be known as the Malcontents. Most of the Malcontents were Lowland Scots who lived near Savannah.

Malcontent—a person in colonial Georgia who opposed the Trustees' rules and restrictions

In December 1740, the Malcontents petitioned King George II and the British Parliament. They demanded the right to own slaves. They made other demands as well, including an end to the limits on how much land they could own as well as the right to choose their own magistrates (government officials who apply and enforce the law).

In the petition, the Malcontents tried to justify slavery and convince Parliament that enslaved people were happy and well cared for:

> *They go through their work with pleasure. They welcome the rising sun with their songs. . . . They are far more happy here than in their own country. . . . it being their masters' interest to take the utmost care of them.*

The wealthy planters in South Carolina were ready and willing to help stir up trouble in Georgia. Residents in

Carolina realized that they, too, would be better off without Oglethorpe and his idealistic system of government. If the Trustees turned over leadership of the colony, Carolinians would have the chance to buy up huge tracts of the best farmland in Georgia and extend their plantation system.

PRESSURE TO CHANGE

Members of Parliament were alarmed at the state of affairs in Georgia. In 1741, they even considered handing over Georgia to the Spanish as a peace offering. The following year, Parliament voted for the first time since Georgia's founding to withhold money from the colony.

The Trustees did, however, take steps to make changes. In April 1741, they reorganized the government of Georgia, dividing it into two separate counties. The Trustees believed that by taking this step, *"we should avoid the constituting one person to govern the whole province, and so preserve the colony to ourselves."* Savannah County included Savannah and northern Georgia. William Stephens, a former Parliament member and the colonial secretary, was named president of this county. Frederica County was made up of Frederica and southern Georgia. While Oglethorpe was there, no president was named. As representative of the Trustees, Oglethorpe was the acknowledged leader of the second county. However, the Trustees asked him to recommend someone to serve as the county's president.

✖✖✖✖✖✖✖✖ P R O F I L E ✖✖✖✖✖✖✖✖

William Stephens

In 1737, the Trustees chose 65-year-old William Stephens to travel to Georgia as their personal representative. Stephen's mission was to have a look at the colony and recommend ways that it could be improved. The Trustees also certainly hoped that Stephens would be able to straighten out some of the problems between the "*clamorously malcontent*" colonists and the Trustees.

When Stephens arrived, he was overwhelmed by the complaining colonists. His journal, kept throughout his stay, was filled with entries such as the one for November 16:

Mr. Bradley came and sat some time with me in the morning, entertaining me with a long narration of his grievances (almost endless to go through the particulars of). . . . Some other persons coming to speak with me put an end to our farther conference. I saw plainly that every hour of my time might be so employed if I showed too much inclination that way.

The Trustees also repealed some of the laws they had made for the Georgia colony. One of the first to go, under pressure from the Malcontents, was the law against importing liquor into the colony. The ban on rum was lifted in September 1742. In colonial times, rum was often used in the trade with Native Americans for animal skins and other goods. Without rum to barter, Georgia's traders had been at a disadvantage.

In early 1743, the Trustees reunited the two counties of Georgia, with William Stephens as president. (Oglethorpe had never recommended anyone to be president of Frederica.) Six months later, Oglethorpe returned to England a sad and bitter man. "*I really believe there is hardly a man in the universe that has had more lies raised of him,*" he wrote to a friend. He would never again see the colony he had founded.

After Oglethorpe returned to England in 1744, he befriended Samuel Johnson, who became famous for being the first person to compile a dictionary of the English language. The aging founder of Georgia Colony is shown here at the sale of Johnson's library.

George Whitefield

George Whitefield, an Anglican preacher from Britain, arrived in Georgia in May 1738. Whitefield was one of a handful of preachers who ignited what historians later called the Great Awakening. The Great Awakening preachers spread the revolutionary message that a person's private relationship with God was more important than membership in any church.

One of Whitefield's goals in speaking throughout the Colonies was to raise money for a new orphanage in Georgia. Whitefield had been invited to preach in the colony by his friends John and Charles Wesley. After he arrived, he decided that Georgia needed an orphanage. Less than two years later, he opened this orphanage, called Bethesda, outside Savannah. *"I think it best to build the Orphan House in the country,"* he wrote, *"because the children will then be near their place of work. For it is my design to teach them by honest labour how to get their own living. It is a constant rule in my house, he that will not labour neither shall he eat."*

A plan of the
Bethesda orphanage

THE MALCONTENTS WIN

In Britain, the Trustees realized that their experiment had been unsuccessful. Georgia had failed to prosper, the morale of the colonists was dismal, and no new settlers were eager to try to make a life there. The Trustees finally agreed to lift the ban on slavery in Georgia in 1750. They also allowed a colonial assembly to meet for the first time. The assembly was made up of representatives from Georgia's towns, settlements, and large families.

In June 1752, the Trustees surrendered their charter to the king. Georgians understood that they now needed to act quickly: They did not want their colony to be annexed by South Carolina, whose leaders wanted King George to grant them more land. Georgians wrote letters to Parliament, asking to remain separate from South Carolina and to become the newest royal colony.

In 1754, Parliament agreed to grant Georgia a royal charter. Under the new charter, heads of households were now awarded 100 acres (40 ha), plus 50 acres (20 ha) for each family member, servant, and slave. The head of the colony's new government would be a royal governor to be chosen by the king. The governor could choose to award a person even more land.

A new lawmaking body was also established. The General Assembly was made up of two houses, a Lower House and an Upper House. The Lower House was made up of 19 men elected by Georgia's male landowners. Only men who owned 500 acres (200 ha) or more could be elected to the Lower House. The Upper House, or Royal Council, was a group of 12 men appointed by the king. As a result, Georgia's new government was controlled by the wealthiest men in the colony.

Released from the restrictive rules of the Trustees, Georgia began to grow and flourish. In 1752, there were no more than 4,000 people in Georgia. Over the next 24 years, that number climbed to about 40,000. During that time, Georgia would be transformed from a struggling settlement to a colony on the verge of prosperity—at least for some people. ✻

CHAPTER SIX

Slavery in Georgia

THE CRUEL SYSTEM OF PLANTATION *slavery becomes a*
fixture in Georgia as colonists buy hundreds of enslaved
Africans to work on plantations.

t the same time the Trustees lifted the ban on slavery, they also passed a series of laws intended to control slavery in the colony. For example, the laws required one white man for every four blacks on a plantation. The Trustees hoped to prevent the population of blacks from outnumbering the population of whites, as it did in South Carolina. This regulation was frequently ignored by white plantation owners. In addition,

OPPOSITE: Successful rice plantations required the use of hundreds of
slaves to engage in back-breaking work so rice could grow unimpeded. In
this woodcut, slaves are loading harvested rice onto a barge which would
travel along Low Country waterways for eventual export to Europe.

the laws banned the marriage between blacks and whites, and any such marriages that already existed became illegal. The law provided for slave owners to be fined if they didn't allow their slaves to attend church each Sunday.

After the ban on slavery was lifted, hundreds of enslaved people were brought into Georgia to work on the big coastal plantations that grew rice, indigo, and mulberry trees for silk production. In 1750, the year the ban was lifted, an estimated 400 enslaved people lived in the colony and about four out of every five people were white. In 23 years, the number of slaves skyrocketed to 13,000, and by 1776, slaves made up about half the population of Georgia.

Savannah became a center for slave trade. At first, slaves were brought to Georgia from other British colonies or islands in the Caribbean. Later, slaves were brought into the colony directly from Africa. Men, women, and children from Africa's western coast, especially the region bordering the Gulf of Guinea, were particularly prized because they knew how to grow rice. The first shipload of slaves from Africa arrived in Georgia in 1766.

The first stop for all enslaved people shipped into Georgia from Africa and the Caribbean was Tybee Island, off the coast of Savannah. The island served as a quarantine station, where slaves were held until they were determined to be healthy and free of disease. Slaves who were sick were kept at the station until they got better or died.

Slave quarters on Georgia plantations were usually simple wood cabins with dirt floors, no windows, and a fireplace for cooking and warmth.

DAILY LIFE

Most slaves in Georgia worked on the large rice plantations that dotted the coastal areas. The method of growing rice in Georgia and South Carolina was brought to the colonies by slaves from western Africa. Life on these plantations was rough. The slaves first had to build extensive networks of ditches and dams to channel the water needed for growing rice. They worked in wet, muddy fields, at the mercy of poisonous snakes and disease-carrying insects. Many slaves died as a result of this hard labor, succumbing to malaria, yellow fever, snakebites, or sunstroke.

Slaves in Georgia usually worked under the task system. When the slaves finished their tasks for the day, they were allowed to tend to their own gardens and families. Despite this tiny bit of freedom at the end of the day, slaves were never allowed to forget that they were owned by their white masters. The slave owner had complete control over every aspect of the slaves' lives. Cruel owners might treat their human "property" no better than animals.

At the end of each workday, slaves went home to tiny cabins with very little furniture. They were supplied with a share of corn as well as any vegetables they grew in their gardens. Some had beds to sleep in. Others had only blankets to separate them from the dirt floor.

From the earliest days of slavery, many people who witnessed the way slaves were treated in Georgia were appalled. One such person was Joseph Ottolenghe, an Italian visiting Georgia in 1751. He planned to teach religion to the slaves, *"these unhappy souls,"* as he called them. In 1759, he wrote a letter describing the plight of the enslaved people he taught:

> *The Negroes . . . loaded with a cruel slavery, ignorant of our language and manners, no idea of our holy religion, . . . loaded with hard labor and worse usages, ill fed, ill clothed, cruelly corrected and barbarously treated, insomuch that a dog and an horse are treated like human creatures when compared with the usages of these poor unhappy wretches are dealt with who first have been robb'd of dear liberty, their native country, beriev'd of their friends, parents, relations, wives and children and at once reduc'd to a most deplorable and cruel slavery!*

Olaudah Equiano

Olaudah Equiano was born around 1745 in what is now Nigeria. He was kidnapped and sold into bondage at the age of 11 and served as a slave to a captain in the Royal Navy. Equiano traveled throughout the world with him and participated in major naval battles during the French and Indian War (see page 80). Equiano was able to save enough money earned from small trades to eventually purchase his freedom. He became involved in the movement to end slavery and traveled throughout the Americas, writing his autobiography, *The Interesting Narrative of the Life of Olaudah Equiano, Or Gustavus Vassa, The African. Written by Himself.* Of his three visits to Savannah, Georgia, before the American Revolution, he wrote that he was always treated poorly. After describing the last occasion, he wrote, *"I thus took my final leave of Georgia; for the treatment I have received in it disgusted me very much against the place; and . . . I determined never more to revisit it."* Equiano died in 1797.

The GEECHEE

SLAVES WORKED TO OVERCOME THE HARDSHIPS OF SLAVERY by building strong communities. Within these communities, slaves tried to maintain bits of their native culture while developing new traditions. In Georgia, slaves on the isolated Sea Islands had the most success in creating and sustaining a unique, distinct culture. These slaves, most of whom were Muslims from western Africa, called themselves Geechee, a tribal name.

Over the years, the Geechee developed unique social customs. For example, newly married couples moved in with the husband's parents until they could build their own home. The Geechee also created their own religious practices, combining both Islamic and Christian beliefs. And they developed a new language, one that couldn't be understood by the white masters. This language combined English and African words. Today, Geechee folklore, songs, and dance are still passed on from one generation to the next.

PUNISHMENT

Because slaves were looked on as property, colonists had no trouble dealing with their slaves harshly. Slaves who worked slowly or were disrespectful were punished. They might be whipped, branded, or beaten.

The colony had special laws for blacks, too. Blacks who broke the laws were treated more harshly than were whites who broke the same laws. Many petty crimes were punished with whippings. But robbery or murder was a more serious matter. Such offenses resulted in death, usually in a gruesome fashion. Hanging and burning were two of the most common ways that slaves paid for such crimes, and it was not uncommon to see a dead slave's head on a pole to serve as a warning to other would-be criminals.

For many slaves, the worst possible punishment was to be sold away from their family. Some slaves were sold off a plantation because they were stubborn or difficult. Other slaves were sold simply because the master needed some extra cash.

Beaten down and treated like animals, many slaves in Georgia took their chances and tried to escape. Alone or in groups, slaves fled to Florida or to the swamps and wilds of frontier Georgia. Groups of runaways banded together, forming their own communities. These slaves were known as maroons, from the Spanish word *cimarrón,* which means "wild" or "savage." Slaves in Georgia would continue to try to escape their fate until slavery was abolished in the United States in 1865. ✻

maroon—an escaped slave who lived with other fugitives in the swamps and wild areas of Georgia and Florida

CHAPTER SEVEN

A Royal Colony

1752 — 1775

GEORGIA BECOMES A ROYAL COLONY *and settlers move into the rugged Backcountry. African slaves teach rice farming to white plantation owners along the coast.*

In 1754, Georgia's first royal governor, John Reynolds, arrived in the colony. Reynolds, a naval officer, was appalled by the conditions in Georgia, especially in Savannah, the colonial capital. Many buildings in the city were falling apart. The first time Reynolds met with his council, part of the government building collapsed. The new governor and his

OPPOSITE: Many poor white Georgians settled illegally on plots of land they found in the rugged Backcountry, far from Savannah. They became known as crackers, an unflattering term thought to come from the sound their whips made as they herded their cattle through dense undergrowth.

lawmakers were forced to meet in a small
shed. Reynolds also considered Georgia's
militia woefully inadequate to protect the
colony. Although the new governor immediately requested
troops and supplies from Britain, his request was thought
too costly and was ignored.

militia—a group of
citizen-soldiers

Reynolds's arrival coincided with the beginning of the
last in a series of armed conflicts between Great Britain and
the allied forces of France and Spain for control of territories in North America. This final conflict would become
known as the French and Indian War. During the war,
many Indian tribes sided with either the French or the
British and their colonists. Many Georgians, especially
those living on the frontiers, lived in fear of Indian attack.

Although John Reynolds was initially welcomed by
Georgia's colonists, he quickly managed to anger the most
influential men in the colony. Reynolds gave the most
profitable jobs to William Little, a close friend who had
accompanied him from Britain. He went against the wishes
of several Georgia planters by failing to investigate
charges of an illegal election that had been held before he
arrived. And he dissolved the colonial assembly when it
refused to do his bidding. Reynolds was finally recalled to
England in 1757.

He was replaced by Henry Ellis, who arrived to
govern the colony in 1757. Ellis, too, was surprised at the
run-down state of the colony. He also realized that

dealing with the unhappy Georgians was not going to be easy. Ellis wrote to the Board of Trade in London, *"I found the people here exceedingly dissatisfied with each other and an almost universal discontent from the late proceedings and persons in power. Few approached me that were not inflamed with resentment and liberal in invectives [verbal attacks]."*

Ellis was an effective administrator. He divided the colony into eight separate parishes, or counties, but was able to unite the bickering groups that had split Georgia politically. He also maintained peaceful relations with the Creek people. However, Ellis's time as governor was short-lived. In 1760, after three years of suffering in Georgia's hot

This drawing shows the back of a typical group of rowhouses in Savannah. They were usually three stories high and less than 30 feet wide. The front entrance was at street level, but house slaves had to use long, steep rear stairways to reach city streets.

climate, he too resigned as governor. Ellis returned to London, where he died three years later.

THE LAST ROYAL GOVERNOR

The French and Indian War ended in 1763, with Britain victorious. The Treaty of Paris (also known as the Treaty of 1763) signed at the end of the war had a very important effect on Georgia. According to the treaty, the colony's southern border was set at the St. Marys River. The western boundary stretched to the Mississippi River, although colonists were not allowed to settle west of the Appalachian Mountains. In addition, Spain gave Florida to the British in exchange for Cuba.

Georgia's third and final royal governor, James Wright, used the end of the war to take control of huge tracts of land. Under the Treaty of 1763, Wright negotiated a land deal with the Creek and the Cherokee that gave him control of land between the Savannah and Ogeechee Rivers. Both tribes had occasionally attacked colonists and their homes during the course of the war. In exchange, Wright promised to forgive any wrongdoing the tribes might have done during the conflict. In no time, settlers were flocking into the newly acquired region, taking chunks of land— with or without permission. Wright called those who took the land without any claim or title to it "crackers."

Popular Governor Wright

Royal governor James Wright would prove to be Georgia's most successful and well-liked royal governor. Born in London in 1716, Wright had migrated to South Carolina as a teenager. In time, the young man became a successful lawyer and was appointed South Carolina's attorney general in 1747. Wright was also a successful plantation owner.

In 1760, Wright replaced the ailing Henry Ellis as royal governor of Georgia. Wright felt right at home among the wealthy plantation owners who controlled the colonial government. While governor, he purchased 11 plantations, gaining ownership of more than 500 slaves and 26,000 acres (10,530 ha) of land. As one of the wealthiest men in Georgia, Wright had a very personal interest in making sure the colony prospered.

By the late 1700s huge rice plantations were thriving along the coast of
Georgia thanks not just to the back-breaking labor of the slaves but also
to the knowledge about rice farming that they brought with them from
Africa and passed along to their white masters.

TWO GEORGIAS

During Wright's time in office, the plantation system in
Georgia continued to grow in size and importance. Since
1750, wealthy slave-owning colonists from South Carolina
and the Caribbean had migrated to Georgia. These new-
comers were given huge chunks of the best land near
Georgia's coastal rivers and Sea Islands,
where they founded massive plantations in
what became known as the Low Country.

Low Country—the
fertile plantation region
along Georgia's coast
and coastal rivers

    Georgia's wealthy planters quickly
came to dominate the colony economically,
politically, and socially. Rice, the most important colonial
crop, became the mainstay of Georgia's economy. By 1768,

Georgia plantations had shipped nearly 17,800 barrels of rice out of the colony. That year, Governor Wright reported that Georgia was making *"a very rapid progress toward being an Opulent & Considerable Province."* Wheat and indigo were also major exports.

Politically, Georgia planters also wielded a great amount of power. Because election to the Lower House was open only to men who owned land or paid a certain amount in taxes, the plantation owners were able to control the colonial government. With a firm hold on the government and the support of Governor Wright, the planters could pass laws that benefited their interests.

The plantation owners used their wealth to create an upper class that hadn't existed in Georgia before. In addition to their plantation homes, they built big brick houses in Savannah that were surrounded by impressive gardens.

LITERACY
in Georgia

MANY OF THE WHITES WHO didn't own slaves in colonial Georgia were illiterate. According to one modern historian, *"Very few wrote letters or kept diaries, and what little is known about their everyday existence is often filtered through elite or non-Southern sources."*

Likewise, few women in colonial times were literate. Many of those who were able to read and write were often too busy to keep a journal or diary of their experiences. What is known of their daily lives must be gleaned from other colonial sources.

Their families feasted on the finest foods and wore expensive silk clothing imported from Europe.

Savannah's merchants also benefited from the change from Trustee to royal government. The colonial port town soon became a center of trade, with lumber, rice, and other goods shipped out of the colony and manufactured goods shipped in. Eager to be a part of Georgia's high society, wealthy merchants patterned their own homes and lifestyles after those of the planters. Soon, Savannah became a center of colonial culture.

With the plantation system firmly in place, the differences between rich and poor became overwhelming. With slaves providing free labor and doing menial tasks, poor whites had fewer job opportunities. And with the wealthy planters and merchants controlling the government, there was little hope for help.

Poor people throughout Georgia did whatever they could to make ends meet. One of the most common occupations was shipping goods along the rivers, from plantations to the port of Savannah. Poor whites also made clothing and shoes, especially for enslaved people. Another common way for poor whites to make a living was to open or work in a roadside tavern or boardinghouse. Some found work as overseers on plantations. For poor women, silk-making, still subsidized by Britain, was a popular occupation.

overseers—supervisors who keep watch over the work of slaves

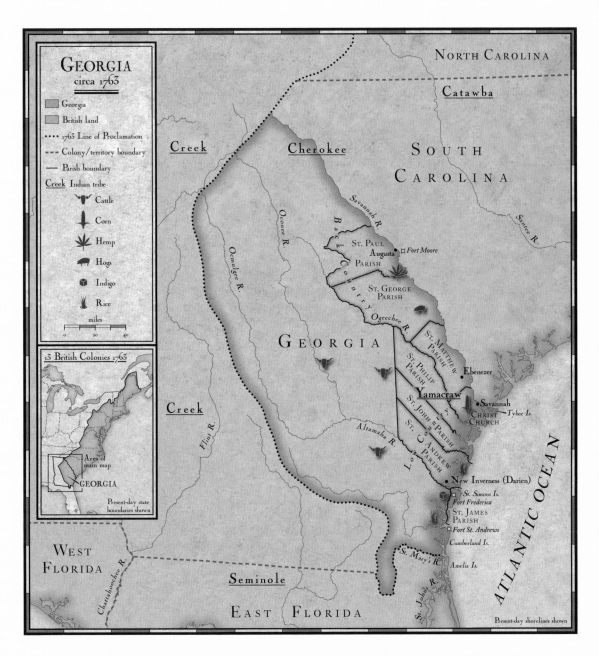

GEORGIA
circa 1763

- ▨ Georgia
- ▨ British land
- ·········· 1763 Line of Proclamation
- – – – Colony/territory boundary
- ——— Parish boundary

Creek Indian tribe

- 🐃 Cattle
- 🌽 Corn
- 🌿 Hemp
- 🐖 Hogs
- ◻ Indigo
- 🌾 Rice

miles

0   20   40

13 British Colonies 1763

Area of main map

GEORGIA

Present-day state boundaries shown

NORTH CAROLINA

Catawba

Creek

Cherokee

SOUTH CAROLINA

Savannah R.

Oconee R.

Oemulgee R.

Back Country

St. Paul Parish
Augusta · □ Fort Moore

St. George Parish

Ogeechee R.

GEORGIA

St. Matthew Parish

St. Philip Parish

· Ebenezer

Yamacraw

St. John Parish

· Savannah
CHRIST CHURCH
Tybee Is.

Altamaha R.

St. Andrew Parish

St. C

Creek

Flint R.

· New Inverness (Darien)

□ St. Simons Is.
Fort Frederica
St. JAMES PARISH

□ Fort St. Andrews

Cumberland Is.

St. Mary's R.

Amelia Is.

WEST FLORIDA

Chattahoochee R.

Seminole

St. Johns R.

EAST FLORIDA

ATLANTIC OCEAN

Present-day shorelines shown

This map shows the limits of Georgia as set by the Proclalmation Line of 1763 after the French and Indian War. The parishes established by Governor Ellis—especially those that made up the Low Country—were the main centers of settlement and economic wealth. As the colony prospered and expanded, the number of Native Americans living in the region dwindled.

Backcountry settlers didn't have the benefit of slave labor. They had to clear the land of trees and dense brush so they could plow, plant, and harvest their own crops. Being good with a gun could save livestock from attack and put food on the table.

GEORGIA'S FRONTIER

Those who settled in the rugged Backcountry, the frontier region around Augusta, were far from the stores, taverns, and coffeehouses of Savannah. These pioneers existed, much as the earliest Georgia settlers had, by hunting and raising livestock.

Backcountry— the rugged frontier region around Augusta

Many of the Backcountry settlers were squatters, people who held no legal title to the land they lived on. They traveled freely on Indian trails and settled on land that the Indians considered their own. In the 1770s, the Indians sometimes attacked and raided these white settlements.

Some groups of Native Americans chose to leave the area altogether. In the 1750s, for example, groups of Creek migrated from Georgia to the northeastern sections of Spanish Florida, settling in uninhabited areas. They became known as the Seminole, a name also derived from the Spanish word cimarrón, meaning "wild" or "untamed." During the American Revolution, the Seminole supported the British against the land-hungry colonists. ※

CHAPTER EIGHT

The American Revolution

GEORGIA IS RELUCTANTLY DRAWN *into the battle between Great Britain and its other American colonies.*

n the early 1770s, Georgia, although growing, was still the most sparsely populated and the poorest of Britain's 13 American colonies. As troubles heated up between Britain and America, many Georgians realized that they had much to lose if war broke out. Family members, neighbors, and lifelong friends became bitter enemies after choosing different sides in the conflict.

OPPOSITE: This painting shows some of the bloodiest fighting that took place as American troops and their French allies made their advance against British forces during the Siege of Savannah in October 1779. Although greatly outnumbered, the British forced the Americans to abandon their attempt to retake the city.

TAXES

Britain's defeat of France in 1763 in the French and Indian War had left her deeply in debt. To protect and preserve the French lands she had gained, the British government decided to garrison ten thousand soldiers in America. To avoid drawing upon the British treasury, it was also decided that colonists should

garrison—to assign troops to a military post

pay for these troops. In 1764, British lawmakers passed laws imposing duties on goods imported into America, including sugar, molasses, and rum. In 1765, the Parliament enacted the Stamp Act, which imposed fees on legal transactions, documents, and many other printed materials (including newspapers and even playing cards).

Although Georgia's merchants and lawyers were upset by the new taxes, colonists there were slower to anger than those in other colonies. As the youngest of Britain's American colonies,

A Plea for
LOYALTY

AN ANONYMOUS LETTER TO THE *Georgia Gazette* in August 1774 explained why one Georgian chose to remain loyal:

Our entering into resolutions against the Government, in the present case, can answer no end but to injure our infant province, by provoking the Mother Country to desert us. Great Britain is our only dependence.

Georgia had the most to lose by breaking with Britain. The frontier colonists counted on British troops to protect them from Indians in the colony, in Florida, and to the west. And Georgia still received funding from the home-land, the only American colony to get this type of help from Britain. The funding was often used to support Georgia's colonial government and to defend the colony.

TIMES OF TURMOIL

In 1774, the Colonies decided to hold a special meeting in Philadelphia. The First Continental Congress was intended to unite the colonists in opposi-tion to Britain. Georgia was the only colony that did not send representatives to the meeting. Georgians were still uncer-tain whether they would be better off without Britain. Governor Wright had recently worked out a second treaty with the Creek and Cherokee tribes. In exchange for paying off the debts that the Indians owed to traders, Georgia obtained even more Indian land.

Continental Congress
the lawmaking body of the 13 colonies during the American Revolution

Wright used his successes to try to keep Georgia's colonists loyal to Great Britain. In January 1775, the royal governor addressed the General Assembly. He said, *"You may be advocates for liberty, so am I; but in a constitutional and legal way. . . ."*

PATRIOT VERSUS LOYALIST

On April 19, 1775, the battles of Lexington and Concord in Massachusetts marked the start of the American Revolution. The idea of British soldiers killing Americans caused many formerly pro-British colonists to turn against Britain. Outraged Georgia Patriots—people who opposed royal authority in the colonies and supported the independence movement— gathered at Tondee's Tavern in Savannah.

Patriot—a colonist who favored independence from England

For more than a year, Tondee's Tavern had served as the headquarters for the Patriot movement. It was here that the Provincial Congress, the Georgia Patriots' governing council, met to plot strategy. After the war's start, the Provincial Congress agreed to send representatives to the second Continental Congress. In addition, the Council of Safety was set up. The council's mission was to hunt down Tories, or Loyalists; seize British weapons and ammunition; and take control of Georgia's military. By the end of 1775, the Council of Safety effectively controlled Georgia's colonial government.

Loyalist—a colonist who remained loyal to England; also known as a Tory

Being a Loyalist in Georgia meant—at the least— being shunned by family members, friends, and neighbors. However, the stakes for Loyalists were often much higher. Some Tories had their goods confiscated, were driven from their homes, or were physically attacked.

A print called "Night attack on the Tories" illustrates a surprise evening attack by Patriot militia on unsuspecting and unarmed Loyalists hiding out in the countryside.

One of the worst punishments suffered by Loyalists in Georgia and other colonies was being bound and painted with hot, sticky tar, and then covered in feathers. Loyalist John Hopkins described his ordeal in a letter:

About 9 of the clock in the evening . . . as I was sitting at supper with my family there came to my house a number of persons (some were in disguise) and opened the door. . . . They consulted to tar and feather me, but the majority resolved to carry me to a more public place. Accordingly they led me into the middle of the square . . . in Savannah and stripped me of

my jacket and shirt and with great reluctance left the rest of
my apparel on me and then they proceeded to tar and feather
me and immediately put me into a cart and carted me up and
down the streets of Savannah for upwards of three hours in
the above condition.

In the crowd that had attacked him, Hopkins identified the town's butcher, two merchants, some mariners and carpenters, a bricklayer, and two "gentlemen."

LOYALIST RAIDERS

Another Loyalist who was attacked by Georgia Patriots was Thomas Brown. Born in Britain in 1750, Brown remained a loyal British subject his entire life.

When the war started, Brown led a small band of guerrilla fighters against the Patriots in Georgia. He called his men the King's Rangers. With the help of Cherokee and Seminole warriors, the Rangers attacked frontier settlements, raiding supplies and burning homes. Later in the war, Brown and his men joined with a regular regiment of Loyalist troops and attacked first Savannah and then Charles Town.

Thomas Brown wasn't the only Georgian who actively helped the British. Other bands of Loyalists fled to Florida at the start of the war. From there, they attacked Patriot plantations and homes, stealing food and other supplies. They were helped by a group of young Cherokee warriors who sided with the British.

In 1776, southern Patriot soldiers turned their attention to these hostile Cherokee, the first tribe to attack the Patriots openly. Their orders were to *"cut up every Indian cornfield and burn every Indian town—and that every Indian shall be the slave and property of the taker; that the nation be [wiped out], and the lands become the property of the public."* Many of the Cherokee who opposed the Patriots were killed or sold into slavery. The remaining members of the tribe signed a peace treaty in May 1777, giving up 5 million acres (2 million ha) of land.

AN ARENA OF WARFARE

The first Revolutionary War battle on Georgia soil took place on March 2, 1776. The bloodless conflict, known as the Battle of the Rice Boats, began when British troops sailed up the Savannah River and captured several ships loaded with rice. The following day, 600 Patriot troops from Georgia and South Carolina took action. They set a ship on fire and cut it loose. The burning ship floated into the captured rice boats, destroying the boats and the rice.

A soldier with the rank of Private in the uniform of the Georgia Continental Infantry (militia)

From August 1776 to July 1778, Georgia's militia, along with Continental Army troops, attempted three separate attacks against British Florida. The attacks were suggested by the Continental Congress, since the region had become a safe haven for colonists loyal to the British.

Continental Army— the troops who fought for American independence during the Revolution under the command of General George Washington

All three of the attacks failed. Heat, lack of food, and disease all played a part in the failures. The Georgians also had to fend off attacks by pro-British Creek tribes and Loyalist spies within their own troops.

In 1778, the tide of war in Georgia turned against the Patriots. Although the British had abandoned the colony in early 1776, they were not ready to give up. After suffering defeats in the northern and middle colonies, British military leaders developed a new plan: to attack the South, the weakest region and the one with the most Loyalist supporters, and move northward from there. As the British advanced through the South, they hoped to attract fleeing slaves and local Loyalists to swell their ranks.

Georgia quickly became a battle zone. As the British struggled to secure Georgia, they burned Patriot homes and destroyed or stole crops and livestock. Later, the Patriots would do the same to Loyalist homes and farms.

In December 1778, the British under Lieutenant Archibald Campbell captured Savannah. In July 1779, royal governor James Wright returned to the colony he had fled two years earlier. For the next three years, he served as Georgia's governor. Georgia was the only colony to have a Loyalist government during the Revolution.

In September 1779, Georgia Patriots tried to take back Savannah. With the help of about 4,000 French troops under the command of Count Charles-Henri d'Estaing (the French had allied themselves with the American colonists in 1778), colonial soldiers laid siege to Georgia's capital. The Siege of Savannah lasted for more than a month. The worst day of fighting took place on October 9, when more than a thousand American and French soldiers were killed. It was one of the bloodiest battles of the war.

During the Siege of Savannah, less than 1,000 British soldiers were surrounded by American troops, aided by 4,000 French soldiers and a cavalry unit led by Polish officer Count Casimir Pulaski. The French Navy is in the harbor beyond.

Throughout 1779 and 1780, the British marched inland and northward, attacking Augusta and other Georgia settlements before pushing into South Carolina. Two important battles in Georgia at this time were Kettle Creek, which the Patriots won, and Briar Creek, which they lost. The British took Charleston, South Carolina, in May 1780. Many southern Patriots fled over the mountains of North Carolina, waiting for a chance to retaliate.

VICTORY AND STATEHOOD

With the British firmly in control of Florida, Georgia, and South Carolina, the Patriots in Georgia could do little except head north to safety or remain behind and wage guerrilla warfare. These Patriot raiders attacked Loyalist plantations, stealing slaves and terrifying the residents. They also attacked and burned rice boats to prevent the food from reaching British troops.

guerrilla warfare—a type of combat in which small groups of fighters carry out surprise attacks against an enemy

In January 1781, General Nathanael Greene of Rhode Island was assigned the task of taking back Georgia and South Carolina from the British. Greene sent troops to Cowpens, a frontier farming area in South Carolina. On January 17, Continental troops and colonial militia decisively beat the well-trained British forces. By April, Continental troops had captured Augusta and begun moving on to other parts of the colony.

In October 1781, Lord Cornwallis, commander of the British Army, surrendered to General George Washington at Yorktown, Virginia. The event marked the end of the American Revolution and victory for the United States of America. In the spring of 1782, the defeated British withdrew from Savannah. One Georgia Loyalist expressed his sadness at the defeat of the British: *"Indeed we may truly say, 'The Glory is departed,'"* he wrote. *"I could weep to think of our situation."*

Georgians now turned to the difficult task of recovering from a war that had left Georgia in worse shape than ever. The Georgia economy was shattered, and the colony's population plummeted after the British left, since many Loyalists and slaves had gone with them. Although Georgia would slowly grow and prosper in the coming years, the wide gap between rich and poor would remain a problem for decades to come.

People who had supported the British during the war did not fare well in Georgia once the conflict was over. More than 270 men who had actively fought for the British—including former governor James Wright—lost their property and were banished from the state forever. Loyalists who were allowed to remain in Georgia were treated with hostility by their friends and neighbors. As the years passed, however, the old wounds began to heal.

During the time of turmoil and instability after the war, Georgia's officials continued to look ahead. In 1785, for example, they chartered the University of Georgia, the first state-sponsored university in the United States. In 1791, officials selected a 630-acre (255-ha) parcel of land on the Oconee River for the site of the new college. The university's first class graduated in 1804.

With the war over and Georgia's admittance to the United States of America in 1788, the city of Savannah turned to rebuilding itself and recreating the charm and beauty the southern port city had been known for.

On January 2, 1788, Georgia officials ratified, or approved, the U.S. Constitution. By signing the Constitution, Georgia became the fourth U.S. state. Although it had been drawn slowly and reluctantly into the cause for independence, Georgia was now ready to be part of a brand-new nation. Georgia officials knew that their state would be better off economically if it joined the United States of America. In addition, the state needed help fighting the natives of the region. In 1786, the Creek had declared war against the people of Georgia to protest a questionable land deal. The Georgians now wanted help defending "their" land.

Georgia's officials were right. In coming years, the plantation system, supported by thousands of enslaved blacks and the Constitution that, at least for the next 20 years, protected the institution of slavery, would allow Georgia to thrive.

TIME LINE

1525 Spanish slaving ships from Puerto Rico visit Georgia to kidnap native people.

1526 Spanish official Lucas Vázquez de Ayllón founds the short-lived Spanish settlement of San Miguel de Gualdape.

1539 Hernando de Soto sets out on a mission of conquest that takes him from Tampa into southwest Georgia.

1568 Spanish missionaries arrive in Georgia to convert native tribes to Christianity.

1685 Spanish missionaries are forced out of Georgia by natives and colonists from South Carolina.

1717 Scotsman Robert Montgomery is awarded land in present-day Georgia but fails to create a colony.

1721 Carolina colonists build Fort King George on the Altamaha River to defend themselves from the Spanish in Florida.

1732 James Oglethorpe and 20 other Englishmen receive a royal charter from King George II to settle the region south of South Carolina.

1733 Oglethorpe and more than 100 settlers found Savannah, the first English settlement in Georgia.

1734 Salzburgers, German-speaking Lutherans, found Ebenezer.

1735 Scottish settlers found the town of Darien. Fort Frederica is founded on St. Simons Island; Augusta is founded at the head of the Savannah River.

1738 Georgia colonists petition the Trustees to allow slavery in the colony.

1740 James Oglethorpe leads an unsuccessful attack on Spanish Florida.

1742 Georgians defeat Spanish troops at the Battle of Bloody Marsh; the ban on rum is lifted in Georgia.

1743 William Stephens becomes Georgia's first president.

1748 A peace treaty ends the war between Spain and Great Britain and sets Georgia's southern border at the St. Johns River.

1750 The ban on slavery is lifted in Georgia; the colony's assembly meets for the first time.

1752 The Trustees surrender their charter to King George II.

1754 Georgia becomes a royal colony.

1760 James Wright, Georgia's last royal governor, takes office.

1765 Britain's Parliament passes the Stamp Act, causing outrage throughout the American colonies.

1774 Georgia is the only colony that does not send representatives to the First Continental Congress.

1775 Battles at Lexington and Concord in Massachusetts mark the start of the American Revolution.

1776 In March, Georgia Patriots turn away British troops in the Battle of the Rice Boats.

1778 In December, British troops capture Savannah.

1779 Patriots fail to force the British out of Georgia during the month-long Siege of Savannah.

1781 British general Lord Cornwallis surrenders to General George Washington at Yorktown, Virginia, ending the Revolutionary War.

1782 British troops evacuate Savannah.

1788 On January 2, Georgia officials ratify the U.S. Constitution, making Georgia the fourth U.S. state.

105

RESOURCES

BOOKS

Blackburn, Joyce. *James Edward Oglethorpe.* Hillsboro, Georgia: Hillsboro Press, 2004.

Cashin, Edward J., ed. *Setting Out to Begin a New World.* Savannah: Beehive Press, 1995.

The Colonial Records of the State of Georgia. Atlanta: Franklin, 1904.

Lane, Mills, ed. *General Oglethorpe's Georgia: Colonial Letters 1733–1743.* Savannah: Beehive Press, 1990.

Scott, Thomas A., ed. *Cornerstones of Georgia History: Documents That Formed the State.* Athens: University of Georgia Press, 1995.

Stein, R. Conrad. *The Conquistadores: Building a Spanish Empire in America.* Chanhassen, Minn.: Child's World, 2004.

WEB SITES

A Creek Indian Bibliography
http://www.rhus.com/Creeks.html
A Web site with links and books about the Creek Indians.

Georgia History
http://www.cviog.uga.edu/Projects/gainfo/ga hist.htm Web site with many links that relate to Georgia's history, including links to historical documents.

Letters from the Georgia Colony
http://msit.gsu.edu/dhr/gacolony/Default.htm This Georgia State University Web site features letters from James Oglethorpe and other early Georgia settlers.

Lost Worlds
http://www.lostworlds.org/index.html
An online interactive museum that focuses on the effect of Georgia's settlement on the Native Americans of the region.

The New Georgia Encyclopedia, History and Archaeology
http://www.georgiaencyclopedia.org/nge/Categories.jsp?path=HistoryArchaeology
A Web site with entries on many aspects of Georgia's colonial history.

Revolutionary War: Southern Phase, 1778–1781
http://lcweb2.loc.gov/ammem/ndlpedu/features/timeline/amrev/south/south.html A Library of Congress Web site featuring documents relating to the South's role in the American Revolution.

QUOTE SOURCES

CHAPTER ONE
p. 17 "Indians...Ochese Creek."
http://www.georgiaencyclopedia.org/
nge/Article.jsp?id=h-579; p. 20 "Now
the friar...killed them all." Scott,
Thomas A., editor. *Cornerstones of Georgia
History: Documents that Formed the State.*
Athens, Georgia: University of Georgia
Press, 1995, p. 3; p. 21 "the English
are...the Catholic religion...." Worth,
John E. *The Struggle for the Georgia Coast:
An 18th Century Spanish Retrospective on
Guale and Mocama.* American Museum of
Natural History, 1995, p. 27.

CHAPTER TWO
p. 29 "useless poor...in Europe." Cashin,
Edward J. *Setting Out to Begin a New
World.* Savannah: Beehive Press, 1995,
p. 8; p. 30 "Our Provinces...and lieth
open." Scott, Thomas A. editor.
*Cornerstones of Georgia History: Documents
that Formed the State.* Athens, Georgia:
University of Georgia Press, 1995,
p. 26; p. 31 "By such...houses and
lands." http://lcweb2.loc.gov/
ammem/ndlpedu/features/timeline/
colonial/georgia/rational.html; p. 32
"We examined...we rejected." Cashin,
p. 24; "for a wife...to labor." Cashin,
p. 8; p. 33 "the most amiable...its
Native Excellencies." Reese, Trevor R.
The Most Delightful Country of the Universe.
Savannah, Georgia: Beehive Press,
1972, p. 7.

CHAPTER THREE
p. 36 "four beef...on their passage."
Reese, Trevor R. *The Most Delightful
Country of the Universe.* Savannah,
Georgia: Beehive Press, 1972, p. 14;
"I went myself...out the town." Lane,
Mills. *The People of Georgia: An Illustrated
History.* Savannah, Georgia: Beehive
Press, 1992, p. 33; p. 39 "The town
of...continual guard kept." Scott,
Thomas A., editor. *Cornerstones of Georgia
History: Documents that Formed the State.*
Athens, Georgia: University of Georgia
Press, 1995, p. 18; pp. 41–42 "Nor
would...might require." Scott, p. 18;
"At our first...very uncouth hollering...."
Cashin, Edward J. *Setting Out to Begin A
New World.* Savannah: Beehive Press,
1995, p. 24; "people greedily...
people." http://specialcollections.
vassar.edu/americana2/merrell-essay.

html; p. 42 "pest...mankind." Wright,
Louis B. *The Atlantic Frontier: Colonial
American Civilization, 1607–1763.* New
York: Alfred A. Knopf, Oglethorpe,
James. 1947; p. 46 "We have...this
country." Oglethorpe, James. *General
Oglethorpe's Georgia: Colonial Letters
1733–1743.* Savannah, Georgia: The
Beehive Press, 1990, p. 393; p. 47 "of
great service...Indian Countrey." Cashin,
Edward J. *Colonial Augusta: Key of the
Indian Countrey.* Macon, Georgia: Mercer
Universtiy Press, 1986, p. ii.

CHAPTER FOUR
p. 51 "The Spaniards...given to them."
Oglethorpe, James. *General Oglethorpe's
Georgia: Colonial Letters 1733–1743.*
Savannah, Georgia: The Beehive Press,
1990, p. 353; p. 52 "mangled...
barbarously." Oglethorpe, p. 420; "die
hard...without fighting." Oglethorpe,
p. 420; pp. 52–53 "I cannot but...by
water." Oglethorpe, p. 536; p. 54
"Having intelligence...amongst them."
Cashin, Edward J. *Colonial Augusta: Key
of the Indian Countrey.* Macon, Georgia:
Mercer University Press, 1986,
pp. 92–93; p. 55 "anonymous young
gentleman." Cashin, p. 98; p. 56 "The
town...account of trade." Cashin, p.100;
"The possum...delicious food." Cashin,
p. 102; pp. 56–57 "I am here...than
daunt me." Oglethorpe, p. 365; p. 57
"the fortifications...falling down."
Cashin, p. 110.

CHAPTER FIVE
p. 60 "The truth was...colony of
Georgia." Cashin, Edward J. *Colonial
Augusta: Key of the Indian Countrey.* Macon,
Georgia: Mercer University Press,
1986, p. 71; "The Darien hath...most
idle." Cashin, p. 418; "I got into...as a
Georgian." Lane, Mills. *The People of
Georgia: An Illustrated History.* Savannah,
Georgia: Beehive Press, 1992, p. 33;
p. 61 "The settlers here...with them."
Oglethorpe, James. *General Oglethorpe's
Georgia: Colonial Letters 1733–1743.*
Savannah, Georgia: The Beehive Press,
1990, p. 372; p. 62 "the use of
Negroes...upon our lands." Oglethorpe,
p. 374; "We humbly beseech...great
inconveniences." Oglethorpe, p. 399;
p. 63 "occasion the...live free there."
Scott, Thomas A., editor. *Cornerstones of

Georgia History: Documents that Formed the
State.* Athens, Georgia: University of
Georgia Press, 1995, p. 35; pp. 63–64
"They go through...their plantation
system." Scott, p. 519–520; p. 64 "we
should avoid...to ourselves." Saye,
Albert B. *New Viewpoints in Georgia
History.* Athens, Georgia: University of
Georgia Press, 1943, p. 86; p. 65 "Mr.
Bradley...inclination that way." Cashin,
p. 60; p. 66 "I really...raised of him."
Oglethorpe, p. 542; p. 67 "I think
it...shall he eat." Oglethorpe, p. 434.

CHAPTER SIX
p. 74 "The Negroes...and cruel slavery!"
Cashin, Edward J. *Colonial Augusta: Key
of the Indian Country.* Macon, Georgia:
Mercer University Press, 1986, p. 119;
p. 75 "I thus took...revisit it." Caretta,
Vincent, editor. *Unchained Voices: An
Anthology of Black Authors in the English
Speaking World of the 18th Century.*
Kentucky, 1996, pp. 238.

CHAPTER SEVEN
p. 81 "I found the...(verbal attacks)."
Cashin, Edward J. *Colonial Augusta: Key
of the Indian Country.* Macon, Georgia:
Mercer University Press, 1986, p. 123;
p. 85 "a very rapid...Considerable
Province." Lockley, Timothy James.
*Lines in the Sand: Race and Class in
Lowcountry.* Georgia. Athens, Georgia:
University of Georgia Press, 2001,
p. 2; "Very few...non-Southern sources."
Lockley, p. 2.

CHAPTER EIGHT
p. 92 "Our entering...only dependence."
Scott, Thomas A., editor. *Cornerstones of
Georgia History: Documents that Formed the
State.* Athens, Georgia: University of
Georgia Press, 1995, p. 42; p. 93 "You
may be...legal way...." Scott, p. 45;
pp. 95–96 "About 9 of the...the above
condition." http://www.cviog.uga.
edu/Projects/gainfo/tar-feather.htm;
p. 97 "cut up every...of the public."
Raphael, Ray. *A People's History of the
American Revolution.* New York:
Perennial, 2002, p.232; p. 101 "Indeed
we may...of our situation." Cashin,
Edward J. *Colonial Augusta: Key of the
Indian Country.* Macon, Georgia: Mercer
University Press, 1986, p.147.

INDEX

ABOUT THE AUTHOR AND CONSULTANT

ROBIN DOAK is a writer of fiction and nonfiction books for children and has authored numerous support guides for educators. Subjects she has written about include American immigration, the 50 states, American presidents, and U.S. geography. Doak is also the author of *Voices from Colonial America: New Jersey*. She holds a Bachelor of Arts degree in English, with an emphasis on journalism, from the University of Connecticut and lives in Portland, Connecticut.

ROBERT OLWELL is an Associate Professor of History at the University of Texas at Austin. He is the author or editor of several books, including *Master's, Slaves, and Subjects: The Culture of Power in the South Carolina Low Country, 1740–1790* and *Cultures and Identities in Colonial British America*, as well as numerous articles on the subject of American colonial history. He has graduate degrees from the University of Wisconsin-Milwaukee and the Johns Hopkins University and lives in Austin, Texas.

ILLUSTRATION CREDITS